CLASSICAL ARCHITECTURE

CLASSICAL ARCHITECTURE

ANDREW BALLANTYNE

THE CROWOOD PRESS

First published in 2023 by
The Crowood Press Ltd
Ramsbury, Marlborough
Wiltshire SN8 2HR

enquiries@crowood.com
www.crowood.com

British Library Cataloguing-in-Publication Data
A catalogue record for this book is available from the British Library.

ISBN 978 0 7198 4165 1

Cover design by Blue Sunflower Creative

Frontispiece: Charles Percier and Pierre François Léonard Fontaine, Louvre, Paris, c. 1812

Image credits
Figs 1, 2, 3, 4, 5, 7, 9, 17, 18, 19, 26, 28, 30, 31, 33, 34, 36, 38, 41, 42, 43, 44, 45, 46, 47, 48, 49, 50, 51, 52, 55, 64, 68, 69, 70, 71, 72, 76, 79, 80, 88, 89, 91, 94, 95, 101, 102, 103, 104, 105, 107, 108, 110, 111 and 112: Shutterstock; Figs 6, 8, 11, 12, 14, 15, 16, 20, 21, 22, 23, 24, 25, 27, 29, 32, 35, 37, 39, 40, 53, 56, 57, 58, 59, 60, 61, 62, 65, 66, 67, 73, 74, 75, 77, 78, 81, 83, 84, 85, 86, 92, 93, 96, 97, 98, 99, 100 and 109: Andrew Ballantyne; Fig. 106: Rolf Hughes; Fig. 90: Gerard Loughlin; Figs 10, 13, 54, 63, 82 and 87: public domain.

Dedication
To J.J. Thomas, who knows where the bodies are buried.

Typeset by Simon and Sons

Printed and bound in India by Parksons Graphics

Contents

Chapter One

Ancient Greece

Starting in Athens

Any building put where the Parthenon is would look important. Held gloriously aloof from the everyday parts of the city, it is on a rocky plateau, the Acropolis, set apart from the rest of the city by cliffs (*see* Fig. 1). The building itself is a wreck. It can be seen from a great distance because of the lie of the land, and these days it is floodlit at night. From far away it makes a good impression, but when we get closer it is obviously no longer in use. The roof is missing, and so are most of the sculptures that used to embellish it. In the digital reconstruction, an idea of the building's shape is restored, but the life is missing (*see* Fig. 2). Nevertheless it has a reputation as one of the world's most beautiful buildings. In part that is because it has the status of a classic. Its beauty is not in doubt. If you do not find it beautiful, then it is your judgement that is at fault, not the building. We are educated to appreciate it.

The Parthenon is one of quite a small number of classical Greek temples to have survived – no more than fifty – some of them with just part of a single column upstanding in place. They are spread across the region that used to speak Greek, but modern national boundaries put them in different countries – the southern Italian mainland, Sicily and western Turkey, as well as the mainland and islands that are now in modern Greece. There are no surviving classical temples on Crete, although the father of the gods, Zeus, was supposed to have been born there.

Not all temples were classical in style. For example there are caves in the cliffs of the Acropolis that were used as temples. This book is about classical architecture, but not all the architecture of ancient Greece and Rome, which under a different heading might be seen as classical periods. Really we know very little about the everyday architecture of the ancient world because it has vanished, but the monumental

Fig. 1 The view shows the Acropolis with the city of Athens in the background. On the Acropolis the ruined Parthenon is clearly visible on the right. The group of sunlit buildings to the left is the Propylaeion – the gateway building – with the small temple of Athena Nike in front of it. Further away, looking smaller and harder to distinguish, the Erechtheion is also visible.

Fig. 2 The Parthenon, Athens, 447–438BCE. Digital reconstruction of the most prominent classical temple.

buildings were more enduring – as they were intended to be. A classical building has columns, or – later – representations of columns. The façades of the Parthenon have columns going all the way round on all four sides. Within the space marked out by these rows of columns there is a closed building with walls that are solid except for a doorway at the end, the *cella*.

Le Corbusier was the most influential architect of the twentieth century. In his book *Toward an Architecture* there is a famous double-page spread with four illustrations that show two Greek temples paired with two vintage cars. The captions explain that we are looking at a temple at Paestum 600–550BCE (a Greek temple, built on land that is now in Italy, *see* Fig. 3) and the Parthenon 447–434BCE,

Fig. 3 The First Temple of Hera, Paestum, c.550BCE. An archaic temple – the oldest one illustrated in this book.

and below them a Humber from 1907 and a Delage 'Grand Sport' of 1921. Le Corbusier's book first came out in 1922 when the second car was brand new and would have looked spectacularly sleek compared with the old Humber, which is a very early car, dating from the year in which Henry Ford produced his first Model T. The idea with the pictures is to notice that the temples differ from one another in the same way as the cars. The older one establishes the type, while the newer one is much more sophisticated and refined.

The temple at Paestum (which the ancient Greeks called Poseidonia) from the early sixth century BCE is now classified as 'archaic'. Its columns are used in the same way as at the Parthenon, going with a steady rhythm right round the building, but their shape is different. They taper much more noticeably as they reach the top, and their capitals spread out very wide. By contrast the Parthenon is called 'classical'. There are other, later buildings in a similar style, but they can be bigger and more ornate, and they are called 'Hellenistic'. The term 'Hellenistic' is used for the period between the death of Alexander the Great (323BCE) and the arrival of the Romans, starting with their conquest of Corinth in 146BCE. There is stylistic development across the 150 years – maybe five or six generations – that separates the temple at Paestum from the Parthenon, but now that another 2,500 years have passed we notice the similarities before we spot the differences.

When Did Architecture Become 'Classical'?

Words keep changing their meaning, so we have to pay attention to when they are being used. At the time when the Parthenon was built, nobody thought of it as either classical or Greek. 'Classical' is a word that was first used by the Romans to refer to the highest class of Roman citizens – it meant the same as 'patrician'. That sense is forgotten in current English, but if we think of 'classical architecture' as originally meaning 'posh architecture' we won't be far wrong. 'Classical architecture' – meaning broadly 'architecture modelled on Greek or Roman style' – was not used in English before the eighteenth century.

'Classical' also has a sense of being the best. Archaic architecture seems to have the right general idea and good intentions; classical architecture is refined and gets it just right; Hellenistic architecture is showy and overdone. I don't want to say that these judgements are right, but to point out that attaching the name 'classical' to a particular period means that we are saying that that period was in some sense the best. The earlier things are finding their way, the later things have lost their way, and the classical works are correct. Other things are judged against them. When we are talking specifically about ancient Greece, 'classical' normally refers to the fifth century BCE, but in a more general conversation it is used to refer to the style of the high-status architecture of that age and everything that has been influenced by it, at any time at all.

'Style' is another word that has changed its meaning. It starts in the Greek word for a column, *stēle*. It is still used in this sense in the specialised language that is used in discussing classical architecture. The row of columns that goes round a temple is called a 'peristyle'. A temple with six columns across its front is called 'hexastyle'. If it has eight, like the Parthenon, it is called 'octostyle'. The temple's base – usually with three steps at its edge going right round the building – is called a 'stylobate', and the columns are placed on it. Buildings without columns are called 'astylar'.

Ancient Greece Was Not a Nation

Another word that has shifted in meaning is 'Greek'. There had been a Greek language from Mycenean times – a thousand years before the Parthenon was built – but never a country with a national border. The word really comes from the Romans, who had the idea of the Greek speakers living in a region (which they called 'Graecia'), but it was not a country with a unified system of government. In the same way, the Romans called the region where German speakers lived 'Germania'.

The Greeks called themselves Hellenes, but other words were used as well. In the *Iliad*, which dates from maybe two or three hundred years before the Parthenon, Homer calls them Achaeans, and by that he means all the Greeks who came together to lay siege to Troy. But the same word is also used to name one of the four ethnicities that the ancient people recognised in the region: Achaean, Dorian, Ionian and Aeolian. These took their names from the sons of Hellen, whose own name has become that of the modern country – *Hellas* in Greek – but English persists in using the Roman-derived 'Greece'.

For architecture, the important groups are the Dorians and the Ionians, who were not well defined in geographical or genetic ways, but came to represent a cultural polarity. The Dorians were portrayed as robust and military, with Sparta the city-state most distinctively associated with them. They were broadly associated with the territories of western Greece. The Ionians by contrast were associated with the east and with the idea of refinement and luxury. Athens belonged to that side of things, the culture being seen to have links with the landmass of Asia Minor (or Anatolia) where the modern nation Turkey now lies.

When the Parthenon was built the city-states were independent of one another – though alliances were made – and there was nothing like the modern nation. Athens was not then the capital city and not the most powerful state. Sparta had greater military power, and when Athens went to war with Sparta, Sparta eventually won (in 405BCE). Thucydides, an Athenian, lived through the years of conflict and witnessed some of the events. He wrote a history of the war, in which he comments that if you were to visit Sparta in the region of Lakonia, then you would think it was just a collection of villages, and wouldn't dream that it had been one of the greatest cities in the world. On the other hand, if you were to find the ruins of Athens, you would think it had been at least twice as powerful as it really was.

His point was that the two places had very different cultures. The Spartans did not have a city wall, because they did not need one. Their military culture was such that if an enemy were to come close, they would be annihilated at a distance, before they ever reached the city. By contrast Athens had defensive walls and monuments a-plenty. There were walls around the city and walls that extended to the coast, so that when there was a siege, supplies could be brought in a protected corridor from the port at Piraeus 11km away. The ruler of Athens (Pericles) gave inspiring speeches that were written down and are still admired, while the Spartans are remembered for their Laconic wit – pithy put-downs backed up with physical menace.

The legacy of Alexander the Great was to spread Greek influence over a vast area south and east of what is now Greece. The Hellenistic kingdoms in these regions were huge and politically independent of one another. Culturally they mixed Greek ways of doing things with more local ways. Some of the greatest monuments of antiquity come from these regions – made possible by the wealth and concentrations of power that gave the rulers freedom to commission lavish buildings.

With the waning of Rome's power, hundreds of years later, there was a greater sense of political centrality in this region, and there was a Greek-speaking capital, Constantinople (as we will see in Chapter 3). In 1453 it was taken over by the Turks, and became the capital of the Ottoman Empire. In those days Athens was a provincial city. The Ottomans used Nauplion as their administrative centre for the region, and it was there that the new king Otho arrived in 1832 to take his throne when the modern nation of Greece was established as a free independent country. The capital moved to Athens because of the splendour of the ruins there, making it the important place that the buildings had all along suggested it was.

The Altar of the Ancient Temple

The crucial part of a sanctuary was the altar. It is here that animals would be sacrificed. Sacrifices pleased the sanctuary's god and obliged him or her to help. In ancient mythology Prometheus made the original people and gave them the secret of fire. He also struck a deal with the gods. He divided up a slaughtered animal and offered the gods a choice between the meat and the rest of the animal – bones wrapped up in the skin. The gods chose the skin and bones, and left the meat for the humans.

That partition of the animal was repeated with the sacrifices at temples in later ages. Animals would be slaughtered, the skin and bones would be burned for the gods, and the humans would cook the meat and eat it. At Corinth there were at least thirty dining rooms in the sanctuary of Demeter and Kore – probably more, as the limits of the site have not been found. The feasts involved far more people than the priests attached to the sanctuary. Most of the meat-eating that went on in ancient Greece was at religious festivals, and feasting could be done in the open air or in temporary shelters (tents, for example) that could come and go without leaving a trace that we can identify.

When Moses was leading his people in the desert, he set up the tabernacle – a formal arrangement of fabric and tent poles – as a portable temple. That would have been during the Greek Bronze Age – roughly a thousand years before the Parthenon. Modern weddings often use marquees for the feast, and the use of temporary awnings need not suggest an informal setting. The solidly constructed formal dining rooms must have been seen as preferable or they would not have been built at all.

The altars in Athens were important in Athens, but had relatively little significance beyond. In purely religious terms the sanctuary on the Acropolis had about the same significance as the temple of Aphrodite on Kythera, or the temple of Nemesis at Rhamnous. They were important for the cult of the particular god, and attracted pilgrims. Nowadays we know where the temples of Aphrodite and Nemesis were, but we have to imagine what they were like. They do not now have the monumental presence of the ruins in Athens.

There were other places that were important to all the different Greek states. The sanctuaries at Isthmia (attached to Corinth) and Olympia held games where athletes from all the Greek states competed. At Epidauros there was an important sanctuary for Asclepios the healer, and people travelled there for the sake of their health. It is now best known for the sanctuary's great theatre (see Fig. 4). The sanctuary of Apollo at Delphi had a more modest theatre and a running track, but it was best known for the oracle who delivered prophecies, the Pythia, and the games that were held here were known as the Pythian Games. It was a site that had great wealth and prestige because it could attract support from many states – there was widespread demand for divine advice.

These panhellenic (all-Greece) sites had the effect of bringing the different Greek-speaking states into contact with one another, forging bonds long before there was anything like a Greek nation with one central government. In each case there was a sanctuary at the heart of the activity, and these sanctuaries were not positioned for their convenience to the citizens of any city-state. There were traditions of divination – reading signs such as thunderbolts, the entrails of animals, or the flights of birds – that continued to be used when a new place was founded.

Often, though, they used places that had already established connotations. For example, at Athens the Acropolis had been fortified in even-more-ancient times and was the basis of a Mycenean settlement from a thousand years and more before the Parthenon was built. Similarly there had been a bronze age settlement at Eleusis, 25km from the Acropolis, which turned into one of Athens' most sacred places – the home of the secretive and theatrical Eleusinian mysteries. The sanctuary at Delphi was on the slopes of Mount Parnassos, where the Muses were supposed to live – they inspired writers, musicians, dancers and astronomers.

Interacting with the Gods

Herodotus (484–25BCE) was from Halicarnassus, a Greek port that remained in the Persian Empire until it was conquered by Alexander the Great in 333BCE. Its provincial rulers had the status of kings, and the most famous was Mausolus, whose funerary monument, the Mausoleum, became known as one of the wonders of the world. That dates from a hundred years or so after Herodotus was writing, so he had no knowledge of it. He is often called 'the father of history' because his writings are thought to be the earliest attempt to write an account of the great events of his time and what led up to them. The great events revolved around the Greeks' success in defeating the army of the great Persian Empire. Although the modern events are explained responsibly in a well-informed way, the background is clearly based in myths and tradition. With Homer's *Iliad* we have a text of uncertain date, but it is assumed to be older than Herodotus by some centuries, and it has history in it that is so interwoven with mythology and poetic fabrication that we cannot read it as a historical account of the events, but rather as a poetic reimagining of them.

One of the striking things about it is how much the gods are involved with the events. Achilles, for example, is not only the greatest of the Greek warriors – he is also semi-divine. His father was the King of Thessaly, his mother a sea-nymph. Helen, who had been abducted by the Trojan prince, Paris, was the most beautiful mortal, but she had hatched from an egg. Her father was Zeus in the form of a swan, her mother either Leda or, in some versions, Nemesis – the goddess of retributive justice. Athena the virgin warrior and Poseidon the sea god were on the side of the Greeks. Aphrodite and Apollo were on the side of the Trojans. Zeus decided not to take sides, but the other gods were in the thick of the action, guiding weapons and inspiring the heroes.

Homer gives us a view of people acting in the world as he saw it. In this world gods and humans are interacting all the time – even interbreeding. The ancient world had no concept of the unconscious, and if you had lived then and felt moved by unexpected emotions then you would think a god had visited. You might appeal to Apollo or one of the Muses for creative inspiration, to a warrior such as Ares (the god of war) or Athena for courage, and if courage or inspiration came, you would know who to thank for it. There were local gods as well, who looked after individual wells or households, and you would want their help too.

The altars at the sanctuaries were the most direct mechanism through which the gods were obliged to take note of human affairs and to intervene in a helpful way if the sacrifices were impressive. Some votive offerings at the temples were small and personal – a clay model of a foot from someone who was lame, for example, or if someone wanted a child they would leave a model of a part of the body that was involved – but the great feasts would be public occasions when the city-state would do honour to its patron god and make sure that she or he continued to dwell in the city and intervene on its behalf. If a city were under siege then the enemy would make sacrifices to the city's patron deity and try to persuade him or her to change sides. For such sacrifices to work the enemy would need to know the god's secret name, which would be closely guarded.

Many altars would have been relatively simple stone platforms, suitable for cooking the meat and burning the rest of the bodies that had been slaughtered and butchered nearby. They could be decorated with sculptures round the sides, and they could be large. They rarely survive because when the old religion was overtaken by Christianity or Islam the old gods were seen as demons and the altars were there to summon them, so the altars were usually destroyed. The altars could be impressive buildings and they could be almost independent of the temples.

The most impressive one to have survived, at least in part, is the one from Pergamon: it is now located indoors in Berlin, instead of being on a high hillside with spectacular views of the heavens above and the plain below (*see* Fig. 5). The arrangement there had the altar slab at its heart, with a sculpted relief on its sides (which is not so well preserved). The altar was set in a courtyard, and the whole courtyard was raised on a plinth, with the surviving sculptures on its sides. It was approached by a flight of steps, and the arrangement allowed the courtyard to be level despite the slope of the surrounding ground. This altar dates from about 300 years after the Parthenon, when Pergamon was the capital of one of the Hellenistic kingdoms. The sculptures depict a mythical conflict – gods fighting with giants – as do many of the architectural decorations in other places. The effect is lively and dynamic, with struggling muscular bodies – quite different from the calm processional mood of the images to be found, for example, on Egyptian temples.

The human body is the constant reference for Greek sculpture, whether it is attached to buildings or standing freely apart. Male bodies are often unclothed, whether in battle or at rest. Female bodies are more often clothed in flowing robes, but there

Fig. 5 Pergamon altar, from Pergamon (now Bergama in western Turkey, near Izmir). The altar is now at the Pergamon Museum in Berlin, 166–156BCE.

are exceptions, especially in the case of Aphrodite, whose name gives us 'aphrodisiac'.

Doric Order

There is a so-called 'dark age' in between the collapse of the Bronze Age (Mycenean) civilisation that built stone palaces and monuments, and the emergence of the civilisation that started to build Doric temples. This dark age did not leave buildings that could be found by archaeologists until in the late twentieth century they started using new techniques. Soil samples were taken into laboratories for analysis with chemical tests, microscopes and Geiger counters. People inhabited the same places during the dark age, but they did not build stone monuments. Post-holes, where timber columns decayed in the ground, can still be detected if the earth has not been disturbed by modern ploughs. The dates for this period are about 1100–800BCE.

The culture that we know about from after that period was certainly different from what was there before it, but there are some lines of continuity. The earliest Greek literature – the poems of Hesiod and Homer – emerge from this darkness, bringing to our eyes (by writing it down) traditions that are assumed to have been passed orally through earlier generations. Before the darkness there was writing, but the surviving documents that have been translated do not amount to literature, so it feels as if in Hesiod and Homer at last there is an insight into how people were thinking. There is in these poems a memory of historical events from the Bronze Age, filtered through understanding that is (in our terms) mythological, and which for them was clearly fundamental. In Hesiod there is an idea of earlier ages of the world that outshone the state of the present – a golden age, succeeded by a silver age, and an age of bronze, followed by the then-current state of the world. So the early world had been populated by giants and heroes who were close to the gods. I imagine that everybody knew this as a fact, somewhere in the back of their minds.

The evidence of early temples is scant and debatable. By later standards they were modest, but they served as a focus for sacrifices, and by about 600BCE there was an established model, which we call the Doric temple. If we look back earlier for an origin, then we are in the realm of contested speculations, but once the Doric temple is present, it seems to carry an authority that makes it something that others wanted to copy, refine and enrich. According to the Roman writer Vitruvius (we will hear more about him in the next chapter), Doric temples were called 'Doric' because they were first noticed in the cities of the Dorians (Vitruvius, Book 4, Chapter 1).

The Dorians were the people who came from the forests of the north and caused the breakdown of the Mycenean culture. Whatever traditions they brought with them would have been hybridised with the local ways of doing things. They learnt Greek. When Vitruvius mentions 'Doric cities' he certainly means cities in Greece, as the Dorians were not known to have left cities when they came to Greece. Their founder, Dorus (Vitruvius says, repeating the suppositions of his time), was the son of Hellen and the nymph Orseis.

By classical times the most prominent Doric city was Sparta, which was known for its austere military culture and communal living. Where architecture was concerned it was known for simplicity. The Dorian zone of influence was centred in the Peloponnese – the main landmass of south-western Greece – with related cities on some islands, in Anatolia (Turkey) to the east, and Sicily and southern Italy to the west.

The Temple of Concordia at Agrigento on Sicily is a good example of the Doric temple type (*see* Fig. 6). It dates from about the same time at the Parthenon, and is almost as well preserved, but we do not know its original dedication. Its value here is that it is typical rather than exceptional. Its shorter ends have six columns, so it is a hexastyle temple. The long sides have thirteen columns, which is the typical proportion – double the number of columns on the ends, plus one. The columns are fluted, so in bright sunlight we see vertical lines running up them. They

Fig. 6 The so-called Temple of Concordia at Agrigento, Sicily, 440–430BCE. The original dedication is not known for certain.

rest on the stone platform – the stylobate – on which the temple as a whole sits. In this case there are four steps running round the edges of that platform; in fact it is more usual for there to be three.

These steps are sculptural rather than practical. In a small temple they can be used in the usual way, but in larger temples they are scaled up. The number of steps does not increase. So a large temple has large steps, which can make them inconvenient for humans to use. Some temples have a stone ramp built, so as to make it possible to move in a dignified way – for example in a procession – between the interior of the temple, where the cult statue of a god would be located, to the outdoor altar where the sacrifices to the god would be made in the line of his or her vision. For example, a stone ramp survives at the temple of Aphaia on the island Aegina. At Agrigento there is not, but there is a temporary modern ramp for the convenience of tourists, and it is possible that a timber ramp was placed here in ancient times when the building was in use.

The bottom of the column is cut off squarely, so it sits on the stylobate with no sculpted base in the column. At the top of it there is a capital – a sculpted 'head' – which in this case looks quite simple. The Doric column always has a capital in broadly this form, but with variation in how much it projects beyond the shaft of the column. The curved form here is called an 'echinus', which is the word for a sea urchin, but the resemblance in not immediately evident, and in English no one ever calls the capitals sea urchins. The same word is used for a hedgehog and the prickly outer casing of a horse chestnut, where the resemblance is clear. It is also the word for a copper bowl, and that is the meaning that best links with the capital. Think of it as a bowl sitting on top of the column. Then the bowl is covered with a flat square slab of stone called an abacus.

The abacus is in between the column below and the entablature above. Think of the entablature as a table top. It takes up quite a substantial part of the height of the building – almost one third of it, if we exclude the slope of the roof, more than half of it if the roof is included. The columns are quite close together – the space between them is about 1.5 column-diameters – so the stone in the entablature does not have to span very far, which is just as well, because stone used as a beam tends to crack in its underside if too much is asked of it. Stone can span much further if it is used as an arch. The ancient Greeks knew about arches, and they are to be found in utilitarian structures such as bridges, but never in high-status buildings such as temples.

The entablature is divided into two main bands. The lower one is called the architrave, and it is absolutely plain. Visually it could be a single beam running along all the column tops, but that would make it a huge piece of stone that would be impossible to manoeuvre into position without it cracking, so in fact it is made up of a series of relatively short (but still very substantial) stone blocks, each of which spans from one column to the next, with joints between them that are so finely made that they disappear from view. Above the architrave there is a frieze, which is panelled, alternating square panels (called 'metopes') with rectangular panels (called 'triglyphs') divided into three by incised channels.

The story that is usually told about this frieze is that it shows in a decorative way a memory of a timber structure. The triglyphs represent the ends of beams. So the correct place for them is directly above a column. There is usually an extra triglyph half way between each column. That is exactly the arrangement here at Agrigento. However, there is a complication. By the classical era – and even by the time of the archaic temples at Paestum – the frieze went continuously round all four sides of the building, whereas beams would have run across the building from side to side. If the triglyphs represent the ends of beams, then we would expect to see them above the columns on the long sides of the building, but on the short sides we should see just the whole length of the beam running across all the columns like the architrave, not the end of it.

So if it is a memory of a system of construction, it is a memory that has become hazy and stylised. It causes a problem for the designer every time the frieze reaches a corner. It does not make sense for two beam ends to be side by side at 90 degrees to one another. Constructionally it would make more

sense if one beam rested on top of the other. What happens, though, is that in order to keep the regular geometry running round the corner, there are two triglyphs there at 90 degrees to each other, but the column at the corner is pulled closer to the next column along, so the triglyph here is not placed centrally on the column beneath it. The space between the last two columns on each side is always a little narrower than the rest. That might be to give the corner subtly more visual strength.

However, in order to keep it from being obvious, the space between the triglyphs here is slightly stretched. The triglyphs stay the same going across the building, but the adjustments are made in the proportions of the metopes, which always look like square panels, but in the middle of the façade they are slightly taller than square, and at the corners they are slightly wider than square. Along the whole of the façade the adjustments are made gradually from one to the next, so the visual effect is of continuous regularity.

We are likely to come away from the building thinking that the columns are regularly placed at the same distance from one another, and that the Doric frieze runs continuously round the building without encountering any problems. We will come back to the Doric temple in an enriched form when we reach the Parthenon below, but it is best understood if we can refer also to the Ionic temple, which is a rather different type.

Ionic Order

The Ionians were associated with western Anatolia – coastal land that is now in Turkey. They looked to an ancestor called Ion who, like Dorus, was a son of Hellen. There is, confusingly, a group of islands in western Greece that is called Ionian (between Corfu and Kythera), but those islands had nothing to do with this Ionia in the east. Three great Ionic temples were built in the sixth century BCE: the temple of Hera on the island of Samos (570–60BCE), the temple of

Artemis at Ephesus (completed 550BCE), and the temple of Apollo at Didyma (540–30BCE).

This area – and indeed the whole of Greece – came to be dominated by the Achaemenid Empire – the Persians, with their capital at Babylon. The Greek cities could be at war with one another, but on occasion they banded together to fight the Persian threat from the east. The political landscape changed when Alexander the Great conquered Persia, and this threat went into abeyance.

The great Ionic temples of the sixth century BCE were the most extravagant and spectacular temples of their time, but they have not survived. The temple of Hera on Samos lasted less than a hundred years, because of either poor foundations or earthquakes, but it was rebuilt, as were the others before their eventual collapse. The Ionic pattern was similar to the Doric. The inner chamber of the temple was surrounded by columns that (with their entablature) were visible from the outside. In the case of these great temples there were two rows of columns right round the building, so the closed room of the temple, with the cult statue in it, was screened from view even more than usual.

The row of columns is called the 'peripteron'. A temple surrounded by columns is called 'peripteral', and these, with a double row, are called 'dipteral'. With a dipteral temple the effect is like a forest of columns, and one comes across the cella, the closed room, almost as a surprise. The cult statue would still have had a direct line of sight to the altar outside, and would witness the sacrifices that were made there.

Column and Capital

Every column comes at a price. There is work in it – skilled craftsmanship – and the materials for it would have to be quarried locally if possible and transported to the site where they would be finished. Increasing the size of the building, and increasing the amount of elaboration beyond the basic idea of it, added enormously to the expense, and these temples were extravagant and magnificent displays. They were in themselves sacrifices to the gods within, consuming the resources of the region that might otherwise have been used for utilitarian things such as food or fortifications. But people thought the temples were worth building. They secured the help of the gods, and they impressed everyone who travelled to visit them.

The columns in an Ionic temple are different from Doric columns. They have a scroll at the top – 'volutes', or two spiral curls. The column also has a distinct sculpted base, and its shaft is fluted with deeper incisions (and there are more of them – typically twenty-four instead of the twenty that are usual with Doric). You could imagine that the flutes in a Doric column are a stylised, neat and geometric version of axe cuts that might have hacked a tree trunk into shape. The Ionic flutes do not look like that. They are definite sculpted deeper grooves. In bright sunlight they make darker shadows than the Doric flutes do, so the columns look more sharply drawn, with fine lines. They are also proportionally taller than Doric shafts – typically the height is eight times the diameter of the column at its base, where the Doric is typically six diameters high. Another difference is in the frieze above the columns. Instead of the alternation of triglyphs and metopes, the Ionic frieze is continuous. It could be plain or sculpted, but it is not divided up into panels so it avoids all the Doric agonies of approaching a corner and adjusting the spacing.

There are two Ionic temples on the Acropolis at Athens. They are much smaller than the great-but-vanished temples in Ionia. In the polarity of ethnicities that made Sparta identify as Doric, Athens identified as Ionic. The Parthenon is a Doric temple and has the robustness and solidity associated with Doric that carried authority in this part of the world, as well as being appropriate to the virgin warrior Athena. 'Parthenos' means 'virgin', and it is that aspect of the goddess that is celebrated in the building's name. However, the building is enriched with things that do not normally belong in a Doric temple, and which are more characteristically Ionic. The two

Ionic temples, though, are the Erechtheion and the temple of Athena Nike. They, too, are unusual in different ways.

Ionic Temples on the Acropolis of Athens

The temple of Athena Nike was completed in about 420BCE, during a lull in Athens' war with Sparta (the Peace of Niceas), but work on it began much earlier, after its predecessor was destroyed by the Persians in 480BCE. The dedication was to Athena as the goddess of victory, and this temple is set on the rampart, so it is very prominent as one approaches the Acropolis (*see* Fig. 7). The gateway building, called the Propylaea, marked the entrance to the sanctuary, but curiously this little temple has a sanctuary of its own – reached through the Propylaea but by turning right and finding a way along one of its wings, rather than going through to the main sanctuary with the other buildings in it.

It is a fine Ionic temple, but with a troubled history, so parts of it are lost. During the seventeenth century, when the Turks were in charge and used the Acropolis as a citadel for the army, the temple was demolished and its stone used in the defences that were constructed here. In the nineteenth century, with independence, the Turkish works were taken apart and the ancient structure was salvaged and reassembled. It has four Ionic columns at each end, but no columns along the sides. This arrangement is called 'amphiprostyle' – 'prostyle' because the columns are in front of the building, and 'amphi' because it is done on both sides (as an amphitheatre is a doubled-up theatre). There is a frieze, parts of which are lost, which ran right round the building above the level of the columns. It depicted people fighting – Greeks and Persians, Athenians and Spartans – as well as gods doing calmer things, such as Athena adjusting her sandal.

The general arrangement of this little temple is rather like that of the treasury of the Athenians at Delphi, but with additional columns. The treasury was built within the sanctuary of Apollo at Delphi to hold votive offerings that had come from Athenians, but also, more importantly, to display trophies seized from the Persians at the battle of Marathon – to

Fig. 7 Temple of Athena Nike, Acropolis, Athens, 420BCE.

remind the visitors from all over the Greek world who came here, that the Athenians had defeated the mighty Persians. The treasury has just two columns, Doric in style, placed between walls – an arrangement that is called 'in antis'. The temple of Athena Nike has two columns in the same arrangement, but screened by the additional row of columns in front.

The treasury, which dates from about 490BCE, was built entirely from marble brought from the island of Paros – a fine material, and costly compared with more local stone. The treasury is close to the entry to the sanctuary, on a path that winds because of the steep slope. Before encountering it the pilgrims would have passed other treasuries and trophies of war, including the figureheads from Persian ships displayed in the stoa of the Athenians – a long narrow building with seven Ionic columns making the whole of one side, so the trophies would be protected from sun and rain, but would have been visible from outside.

The stoa was an adaptable building type and was used in various ways. Traces of these buildings are often found in sanctuaries with a row of dining rooms behind the colonnade. In the Agora at Athens, which is just below the Acropolis, there were several – built to establish the edges of the space with their long straight lines, after centuries of it being a space with no very defined shape to it. In one of them, the Stoa Poikile – the painted stoa –a school of philosophy (the Stoics) conducted its business. Another, the Stoa of Attalos, dates from rather later and is now very prominent on the site because it was reconstructed in situ in the mid-twentieth century (*see* Fig. 8). Attalos was a king of Pergamon, educated in Athens and who gave the building to the city.

Looking up from the Stoa of Attalos today one can see the Ionic portico of another temple on the Acropolis. This is the Erechtheion. There is nothing like it. It has an irregular plan-form, which seems to be because it had to make adjustments because of the special things to be accommodated here. For example, there was an open courtyard with an olive tree growing in it, reputed to be a direct descendant of the original olive tree that Athena had presented to the city – one source of the city's prosperity.

The other main source was the sea, and there was a story – again we are in a realm where history and myth cannot be separated out – that at the foundation of the city there was competition between Athena and Poseidon to be the city's patron. Athena won, of course, which is why the city is named after her, but

Fig. 8 The Stoa of Attalos, Agora, Athens (the long building on the right of the open space of the Agora, seen here from the Acropolis), 159–138BCE.

the mark of the competition that remained was a scar left in the rock by Poseidon's trident in the form of a thunderbolt. This threefold mark is framed in the exposed rock surface of the porch of the Erechtheion that looks out over the Agora. Finally the building is named after Erechtheus, the city's founder and king, who was raised by Athena and who was buried here on the Acropolis, and the building could not encroach on his tomb.

Inside the Erechtheion there were treasures, including an ingenious folding stool made by Daedalus – his work on Crete included the device that made possible the conception of the Minotaur, as well as the labyrinth in which the Minotaur hid. He was eventually slain by Theseus, who became king of Athens. There was also a stove with a chimney in the form of a palm tree that was attributed to Callimachus, who was later credited with inventing the Corinthian capital (*see* Chapter 2). And there was an old cult statue of Athena, which was revered, even when the much larger statue by Phidias was set up in the Parthenon across the rock.

There were three porches to the building, each with six columns, but they are all different. The first, which I mentioned above, frames the mark of Poseidon's trident, and it has four columns across in a row, with two set behind the columns at each end of the row. This porch is almost freestanding and may not have connected into the rest of the building. At the west end of the building the six columns are in a single row across the front, in the same prostyle arrangement as at the temple of Athena Nike. This would have been the building's entrance, and I imagine that the statue of Athena Polias would have been put on axis with it, so she could see out to the altar – though there is ancient mention of the rites at this temple involving indoor sacrifices.

On the south side of the building there is another porch, but this does not allow an approach from the outside. There are stairs to reach the space from within the building. The columns here are arranged as on the north side, with four across and two tucked in behind, but this porch does not align with the other – they are almost on the same axis, but they are very different sizes, while the columns of the south porch are carved to look like young women balancing the entablature on their heads. It is called the Porch of the Maidens (*see* Fig. 9).

All in all the building is a puzzle. We do not know exactly what went on in it, but it was a building of the highest prestige. It was beautifully carved with decoration that enriched the standard Ionic order

Fig. 9 The Porch of the Maidens (Caryatid Porch), Erechtheion, Acropolis, Athens, 420–406BCE.

as well as the doorframes and suchlike. There was a sculpted frieze, in a darker stone with lighter figures attached to it, and the whole building was painted, coloured and picked out with gilding and coloured glass used like gemstones. Architecturally it shows that although the regular disciplined temple form was the norm, it was not the only building design that was acceptable for a place of the highest status.

The Parthenon

Where the Erechtheion contained the city's most precious religious treasures, the Parthenon was the great artistic showpiece. It is much the largest building on the Acropolis, and it was commissioned as a display of confidence after the Persians had been routed. The Persians had demolished an earlier temple here, and its rebuilding – more magnificent than ever – after the Persian defeat was symbolically important. At first glance the Doric temples tend to look much the same as one another, but in fact each has its peculiarities. The Parthenon is unusually impressive not only because of its site, but also because it is much larger than the others. There is a temple down in the Agora for example, the Hephaesteion, which is in some ways much more typical. Its columns are about half the height of the Parthenon's, it has six columns across the front compared with the Parthenon's eight, and it is not built in marble, so it is less sharply defined in bright sun.

The Parthenon contained a famous statue of Athena, by Phidias – whose statue of Zeus at Olympia was considered one of the wonders of the world. The statue of Athena was not far behind. She stood with her shield resting on the ground, sheltering behind it a python – symbolic of an older religion – and encrusted with symbols of one sort and another that show the older cults subsumed within her great all-encompassing power.

The cella in which she stood was lined with two rows of Doric columns, one above the other, and the space's natural light would have come from the open door – which would have been adequate, as the sunlight here is intense, and even in modern houses the shutters are often kept closed across the windows all year round. Even a small crack allows in enough light. One of the unusual things about the Parthenon is that the cella has a second chamber, entered from the outside at the other end of the building. It is thought to have been the city's treasury – valuables being kept in this fortified and well-secured zone, protected by the fear of sacrilege as well as by physical barriers. In this chamber there were four Ionic columns supporting the roof – the tallest columns in the building.

Outside the building, above the Doric columns, there was the normal type of Doric frieze, with particularly finely sculpted metope panels showing centaurs, Amazons and giants fighting with Greeks. Then in addition to that, there is a frieze that runs round the outside of the cella. This is like the frieze of an Ionic temple, except that it is tucked away behind the columns instead of being in full sunlight above the columns. It is an extraordinary embellishment, and it shows a procession with varied groups of people, some on horses, bringing the sacred cloth to drape round the statue of Athena in the Erechtheion. This fabric was replaced every four years, brought in procession from a temple at the city wall.

Entasis

The work involved in making the temples was always meticulous, but at the Parthenon it was obsessive to an unusual degree. All the building lines that one assumes are straight are in fact very gently curved. Apparently this is to prevent the optical illusion that would make it look as if the horizontal lines slightly sagged if they were actually built straight. So the whole platform on which the Parthenon is built is very slightly domed, and the columns, which all taper, have a slight bulge in their tapering. This optical refinement is called 'entasis', and it is not found in all temples. This highly skilled work would not sustain a mason through a working life. Even Athens did not need top quality masons all the time. Once the Parthenon was built, it was built. There was no immediate need for another one, so the people in charge moved around to places where their skills were needed.

The Temple of Apollo at Bassae

One such place was Bassae, where some of the people who worked on the Parthenon were subsequently employed. Ictinus is credited as the architect. It is an extraordinary temple, not least because of its location in Arcadia, in remote hills not close to any major cities (*see* Fig. 10). The temple was evidently commissioned

Fig. 10 The interior of the temple of Apollo Epikourios, Bassae, 450–400BCE; reconstruction drawing by Charles Cockerell, 1860. The depiction of the stonework is accurate up to the level of the frieze. The cult statue here is placed to make sense of the east-facing doorway, but the surviving stone paving suggests that the statue of Apollo would have been placed in front of the central column. The roof light is not plausible.

to give thanks for an escape from plague, and it was dedicated to Apollo the helper – Apollo Epikourios. It is not as large as the Parthenon, but it is still a remarkable thing to find in a small farming community. The design seems to pick up on local traditions, which made samples longer and narrower than elsewhere. The six columns across the front go with fifteen along the sides (rather than the thirteen that would be expected).

The orientation is unusual, with the main axis running north–south, rather than east–west. Looking out through the main door, one looks north, so the cult statue would never have seen the sun directly. There is a second door, in a subsidiary space separated from the main space by a row of columns. The space has a door that looks out to the east, to the rising sun, which is to be expected. The columns round the outside of the building are Doric, but the interior space is a departure from the usual formula. Instead of columns there are piers – projecting walls – with the ends sculpted so as to make them look like columns. They have capitals that are Ionic in character, but they do not follow the usual pattern. They are not found elsewhere in the ancient world.

Most remarkably of all there was a single column in the middle of the screen separating the two chambers, with a capital that came to be known as Corinthian. This is the oldest known example of it. It might have been the first, but there could very easily have been others that are now lost. The oldest one found on the outside of a building is on the choragic monument of Lysicrates at Athens – a monumental support for a trophy (a tripod) won by the chorus sponsored by Lysicrates (who is not remembered for having done anything else, *see* Fig. 11). The Corinthian capital became a canonic type and was used very prolifically by the Romans. But here it is, in the depths of the countryside, apparently before it was used anywhere else.

It is unusual to find a column placed on-axis as it is here, as well as it being the only example of a different order being used for a single column in a building that has other columns in and around it.

Fig. 11 The choragic monument of Lysicrates, Athens, 335–34ʙᴄᴇ. The acanthus leaf decoration at the top originally supported a tripod, which was awarded as a trophy in competition and proudly displayed.

Some of the archaic temples had an odd number of columns in their entrance façade, but it seems awkward because it puts a column in the middle of the doorway and blocks the sightline of the cult statue. The arrangement at Bassae makes the Corinthian column look like a focus of attention, rather than being part of a frame. There is a tradition of using a central column as a sculptural focus that goes back at least as far as the so-called Lion Gate at Mycenae – a thousand years or so before the Bassae temple. In a panel above the main gate to the citadel at Mycenae there is a relief showing a column with a capital and a base flanked by lions. The column used in this way can be emblematic of protection – it stands as a sentinel – maybe here just behind the cult statue, which was revered but taken away from this location to the city of Megalopolis that grew up later in this region.

When we visit the site today, we tend to appreciate the scenery and imagine that the site was chosen because it was so beautiful and impressive, but there is nothing in the ancient texts that encourages this view. Normally when the ancient Greek authors had anything appreciative to say about natural landscape it was because there was a cool spring or the shade of trees – something to make people comfortable. What mattered most was the connection with the gods – is the site auspicious? Will we be able to reach the gods through sacrifices at the altar if we place the altar here?

Established Orders

What we see in ancient Greece is the development from obscure origins of a way of designing high-status monuments that became very codified and obsessively refined. This did not happen equally everywhere. Often fine buildings were commissioned because there was a concentration of enormous wealth, so people could afford them. In the case of Bassae, though, and not only there, there was a determination to have something of the finest quality and magnificence, even though it must have stretched the resources of the community. Bassae is on the Peloponnese and was closer to Sparta than Athens, but its values look more Athenian than Spartan.

In Sparta the building of fine monuments was seen as pointless waste, and nothing of great note survives. There is the ruin of a large monument to Menelaus – the Spartan king who married Helen and whose life belongs in mythology as much as history – but there is nothing fine about it. It has the form of an earthwork regularised with masonry. Excavations around it have unearthed many votive offerings, so it was actively used as a place of worship.

In the Parthenon there is, by contrast, a level of refinement that went beyond anything that had been achieved before, both in the sophistication of the optical refinements, adjusting the slight curvature of every major line, and in the beauty of the sculptures of the two friezes and the effigy located within. By the time the Romans invaded and started to rule this region, they too could appreciate the architecture's achievements in giving an impression of authority and good order.

Chapter Two

Ancient Rome

Concentrations of Power

If I try to build by myself, I don't get very far. My energy and my money are soon used up. For great monuments to exist there have to be concentrations of power, so that the work of many people can be directed towards one project. When people are nomadic and wander as hunter-gatherers, they do not build anything much. Permanent settlements were first made in Mesopotamia – on land that since 1922 is mainly in the modern country of Iraq. The concentrations of wealth produced by agriculture and slavery made possible such structures as the Great Ziggurat of Ur (twenty-first century BCE, restored sixth century BCE and again in the late twentieth century) – a 30m tall structure made from sun-dried clay bricks. In Egypt the communications along the length of the River Nile made it possible for a single ruler to command a very long narrow territory, and the rulers of Egypt built enormous structures in stone – for example the great pyramids and temples.

When Rome was founded in 753BCE (as tradition has it) it was at first a city-state at the southern edge of Etruria and it had Etruscan kings. In 509BCE there was a revolution and the kings were overthrown, to be replaced by the Senate. The Roman Republic had aggressive policies and annexed nearby territories, then looked further afield. For example the Greek city-state of Poseidonia was founded about 600BCE about 300km from Rome, and its temples were built soon after; but then it fell to the Lucani in about 400BCE, and then all the Lucani lands were taken over by Rome in 273BCE, when Poseidonia's name changed to Paestum. Its monuments (*see* Chapter 1, Fig. 3) were more impressive than anything in Rome at that

time. The greatest Roman monuments date from rather later, after the murder of Julius Caesar, when the republic declared itself an empire. Augustus, the first emperor, ruled from 26BCE–14CE and he transformed the city of Rome – according to Suetonius, Augustus said that he found Rome as a city of brick and left it as a city of marble.

The most delicately beautiful monument in Rome is the Ara Pacis – the Altar of Peace – which is the altar associated with the mausoleum of Augustus, where he and his family were buried. The details of the altar show in pastoral scenes the animals that were sacrificed there, and the central part around the place where the slaughter took place is decorated with ox skulls and festoons of flowers carved in marble. One can imagine that earlier altars might have been decorated with real ox skulls and real flowers, but obviously they have long vanished and the Augustan marble has survived (*see* Fig. 12).

Later emperors also commissioned lavish works, and over generations the city became spectacularly enriched with monumental buildings – but it also became difficult to rule. In 330CE the emperor Constantine founded a new Rome in the east at Byzantium, which he renamed Constantinople (now Istanbul). Rome fell to barbarian invaders – Vandals, Huns, Goths and Visigoths – in the fifth century, with the Sack of Rome in 410CE, and the empire's influence in the west was by then very diminished. In the east, the Greek-speaking emperors at Constantinople continued to develop their Roman traditions for another thousand years, as we will see in Chapter 3.

During the time of the empire the Romans controlled territory that included everything round the Mediterranean, as well as North Africa, and territory as far north as Britain and much of the former Persian

Fig. 12 Ara Pacis, Rome, detail of sculpted decoration. 13–9BCE the Altar of Peace, associated with the mausoleum of Augustus. The decorative ox skulls (*bucrania*) and festoons of flowers probably show how earlier altars had been decorated for festivals.

Empire's land in the Middle East. The Romans were great builders. The empire was held together by its communications, which depended on the network of sea routes, roads and bridges that enabled relatively high-speed travel – on ship, on foot or by horse. Food was grown where the conditions were good for growing and brought to where it was needed, and water diverted, sometimes through aqueducts, to serve the great cities.

These infrastructures stretched across the empire and kept things working, along with the army-supported administration that kept people in order and dispatched trouble-makers. The poet Juvenal coined the phrase 'bread and circuses' to describe the needs of the general populace: basic necessities and distractions. The Roman state built not only temples but also administrative and entertainment buildings in the provinces as well as in Rome itself.

The Unique Legacy of Vitruvius

We have much more insight into the building culture of the Romans than of the Greeks because of the survival of a text: the ten books of architecture by Vitruvius. For the modern world he is uniquely important, because his is the only ancient treatise on architecture that we have. There are some fragments by other writers, but nothing comparable. As a commentator he was not ideally placed. He was from Rome, travelled widely – possibly with Julius Caesar's army in Gaul – and elsewhere, including Greece where he seems to have spent most of his career. He was working at the beginning of Augustus' reign, but died too early to see the transformation of Rome – still less the grandiose structures that are for the modern world Rome's best known ruins.

However, Vitruvius worked as an architect and was steeped in the culture of the profession at that time. The reason that his work survived is because it was copied many times – all books were handwritten in those days, on rolled scrolls rather than pages – so people wanted to use the books, and his might well have been the pre-eminent text on architecture in ancient times.

Having said that, his work may have been read less for its practical advice than for its semi-mythical content about the origins of things. Ordinary transmission of the practical skills involved with building did not occur through reading books. There is no ancient treatise on woodwork, for example, not because there was no culture of craftsmanship involving timber, but because it was not a literary tradition. Joiners may or may not have been literate. In the same way that recipes for domestic food would traditionally have passed from mother to daughter, and techniques would have been learnt in the home, so the guilds and apprenticeship systems ensured the development and passing on of skills without the need for books.

Vitruvius is often, without doubt, a reliable guide, and his insights about Greek architecture have often been followed in later centuries. How did the Corinthian capital originate? There is no way for us to know for sure, and any direct archaeological evidence is unlikely to resolve things. But Vitruvius tells us that it was invented by Callimachus, a Greek sculptor. He found the grave of a young Corinthian woman, on which her nurse had placed a basket containing the girl's personal things. To protect them the nurse put a roof tile on top of the basket. She did not notice that she had put the basket on top of the root of an acanthus plant, and when spring came it grew up around the basket. When Callimachus saw it, he was charmed by it and sculpted it in marble (*see* Fig. 13). The proportions of the columns that bear the Corinthian capital are supposed to be more slender than the other orders, says Vitruvius, so they resemble the proportions of the body of a young woman. By contrast the columns of a Doric column should be sturdy like a soldier, the height being six times the diameter of the base, as a man's height is six times the length of his feet.

Vitruvius explained and codified the differences between the orders of architecture – the Doric, Ionic and Corinthian – which he certainly did not invent, but which we would not know about with such clarity and certainty had his text not survived. The differences between Doric and Ionic were there to be inferred from the archaeological evidence, but it is not clear that we would have known that these had been their names since antiquity. Following

Fig. 13 Callimachus inventing the Corinthian capital. The story was told by Vitruvius, who died in 15BCE. The illustration is from much later Fréart de Chambray, *Parallèle de l'architecture antique avec la moderne* (Paris 1650).

Vitruvius in seeing the columns as figures, we can imagine a phalanx of sentinels around the abode of the cult statue in a temple. The single place where the columns are actually modelled as figures is the Porch of the Maidens in the Erechtheion (*see* Fig. 9), though Vitruvius mentions another important example that has not survived. That was a porch in the Agora at Sparta, where, after the battle of Plataea, the columns were modelled as Persians, to show the Spartans' defeated foe enslaved in the unrelenting task of supporting the entablature.

The female figures at the Erechtheion, says Vitruvius, were Caryatids, named after the inhabitants of Carya – a Greek town on the Peloponnese that had sided with the Persians. We would not have known this without Vitruvius, and it is far from certain that his information was correct. The statues do not look downtrodden in the way that the story would suggest, so people who write wanting to avoid making this assumption call the porch the Porch of the Maidens – but the rest of the world follows Vitruvius and calls them Caryatids, along with all other sculpted figures, especially female figures, that act as columns. This blend of the mythical with the plausible-but-unverifiable is to be found not only in Vitruvius, but also in official buildings.

Temples of Ancient Rome

The Temple of Vesta

The Temple of Vesta in Rome was one of the oldest and most sacred places. Vesta was the goddess of the hearth, and in the temple there were relics that had been brought to Rome by Aeneas, a Trojan prince, when he fled Troy after the Greek attacks. Aeneas was mentioned by Homer in the *Iliad*, and Virgil made him central in the *Aeneid*, which was written during the time of Augustus and helped to make the rule of the Caesars seem legitimate because they claimed descent from Aeneas – whose mother, by the way, was the goddess Venus. In a Roman house there would be a shrine with the household gods. A flame would be kept alight there, and if it went out there was a superstitious belief that there would be a death in the household. The shrine of Vesta was the hearth of the city, and a flame was kept burning there, tended by the Vestal priestesses. If it was allowed to go out then the priestesses would be put to death, in the hope of averting the wider catastrophe signalled by the incident.

The old part of the Roman Forum where the Temple of Vesta was to be found – a temple with a circular plan – also had the Temple of Romulus, the foundation temple for the city, founded by Romulus, who was abandoned with his brother Remus: the two were suckled by a she-wolf in this vicinity. So there are two foundation stories side by side – one for the inauguration of the city, the other for the arrival of a special destiny with Aeneas and the Trojan spirit – made real and evident through being present in monumental buildings.

The Old Roman Forum (*Forum Romanum*)

The building that came to dominate the old Roman Forum was the Basilica Giulia (or Julia – there was no 'J' in Roman Latin) initiated by Julius Caesar and completed by his adoptive son and successor Augustus. It was a basilica – a large building with an official character. As a building type it developed from the Greek stoa, the long narrow buildings with columns along one side – here a royal stoa (basilike stoa). Cato the Elder built a monumental stoa in the forum, the Basilica Porcia (184BCE), accidentally destroyed by fire in 52BCE, soon after the nearby Basilica Sempronia had been demolished to clear a site for the Basilica Giulia. The Roman examples, like the Greek stoas, were quite open buildings with interiors that were shady and therefore more comfortable than the outdoor space of the forum. They were used for conducting business, and – more formally – for legal trials and political speeches.

The last monumental basilica to be built near the forum was the Basilica of Maxentius (completed by Constantine, 312CE), and parts of it still stand (*see* Fig. 18). It was made with huge vaulted spaces, and was dominated by a colossal statue of the emperor, so very clearly it had an official character; the original meaning – a 'royal presence chamber' – is evoked with the divine or semi-divine presence of the ruler presiding over the trials and business being transacted there. A significant role for architecture in the Roman Empire was to establish the character of Roman rule throughout the empire's provinces, and every town would have a basilica commensurate with its status. In Rome they were grandiose, while in small towns they were modest, but would carry the mark of classical style – some routine classical columns at the porch.

Notable Structures of Ancient Rome

Typical Roman Temples

There were strong connections between the Greek style of monumental architecture and that of the Romans, but also some differences. For example, Vitruvius tells us about the Etruscan temple. It was, like the Greek temple, built on a stone podium, but unlike the Greek temples, which usually had three steps going all the way round, the Etruscan temple had steps on only one side, and the number was not an issue. There were steps that were the right size to walk up, and there were enough of them to reach the level of the temple.

The columns were made of timber, and proportionally there was much more space between them than with the stone columns of the Greek temples, and they were across only the front of the temple (prostyle). The walls were made of mud brick so they were vulnerable to rain, and were protected by the roof, which had a pronounced overhang on all sides. The columns were plain – unfluted but with a simple capital rather like the Doric, and a base more like Ionic than Doric. Vitruvius calls this column type the Tuscan order. The Romans tended to use this Tuscan order for relatively modest buildings that needed an air of dignity, and the Corinthian when they wanted a show of magnificence. In multistorey buildings different orders might be used on different levels of the façade.

The Maison Carrée at Nîmes

The temple at Nîmes, called the Maison Carrée, has an exceptionally well-preserved outer shell and shows very clearly the type of temple that the Romans built in the centre of their provincial cities (*see* Fig. 14). Nîmes was important, and the temple here is better than ordinary – a fine and splendid work – but typical in the way it drew on earlier temple types. It dates from about 2CE, during the reign of Augustus, and it was dedicated to Gaius and Lucius – grandsons and nominated heirs of Augustus – who died as teenagers just before the temple's dedication.

The temple is on a storey-high plinth, and the cella goes right across it, as in the Etruscan temples. The spacing of the columns is just as it would be in a Greek temple, but here the six columns across the front and an additional two on each side are the only ones to be

Fig. 14 Maison Carrée, Nîmes (consecrated 2CE). The best preserved Roman temple of the 'standard' type.

fully modelled. They have Corinthian capitals, as do the pilasters that decorate the sides of the building. These look at first as if they are columns, but they are fairly flat sculpted representations of columns. Structurally they do not act as columns. They are decoration on the wall. Instead of the capital being carved in the round as acanthus leaves sprouting and curling around a basket, we see just one side of the arrangement, as if the rest of it is lost within the thickness of the wall behind. This arrangement is called 'pseudoperipteral' – it looks at first glance as if the temple is peripteral, with a row of columns running all the way round, but it turns out that most of them are not structural columns at all, just decorative pilasters.

In constructional terms, this is a major theme of Roman building. The columns and beams of the Greeks were seen as 'admirable'. Usually, though, in Greek buildings a column would act as a load-bearing post, supporting the stone beam that ran across the top. In Roman buildings the admirable columns were used to give the buildings an air of grandeur and respectability, but they were often not structural at all, but just an embellishment. Roman structures made much greater use of the arch to support things – something the Greeks had known about

in principle, but that they avoided when they were trying to impress.

The Pont du Gard

Near Nîmes there is one of the greatest of Roman utilitarian structures, the Pont du Gard (*see* Fig. 15). The bridge crosses a small river, the Gard, 24km away from the Maison Carrée – well outside the city. The river here is in a valley with steep sides, and the bridge was there to carry a water channel across the valley, to supply the city with extra water. It is impressive. Three tiers of arches are arranged on top of one another, to support the water channel, which runs absolutely straight, with an even imperceptible slope, so the water can run without the need for pumping, drawn along by gravity. It is an astonishing achievement of ancient engineering. The stones were all moved into position by human effort and ingenuity, supplemented by beasts of burden for some of the heavy lifting.

The stone that we see is just part of the building operation. The core of the structure is concrete, which set hard and became immensely solid and permanent. The stone is a casing that was built to

Fig. 15 Pont du Gard, near Nîmes (40–60CE). An unadorned arched structure, which never had the overlay of classical ornament that the Romans would have given it had it been seen as a monument.

hold the concrete in shape. It acts as a shuttering. In a modern building that you can see is made of concrete there was some shuttering to mould the concrete before it set, and normally it is taken away. Here at the Pont du Gard it was left in place, as was intended.

There is also another building operation that was always designed to be temporary. An arch supports itself once it is complete, but before it is complete there has to be something to hold the stones in position. That is usually timber 'form-work' or 'centering', which is robust and reusable. It would go up like a sort of scaffolding, supported on stonework that had already been built. The arches would be arranged, and concrete mixed and pounded into position. Then when everything had set, the timber could be removed, and used to set up another arch.

The stonework in the Pont du Gard has blocks that project from the vertical face of the bridge. They would have been used to support the temporary timbers when the bridge was under construction. If the structure had been designed as a more polished work with artistic pretensions then these projections would have been trimmed off (and probably the whole bridge would have been covered in sheets of marble) – but they are still in place today. The bridge was seen as a utilitarian structure that did not need a polite finish so long as it did its job.

Fig. 16 Amphitheatre, Nîmes (70CE). This important building in the city centre has arches and vaults to hold it up, but they are decorated with the classical ornament of columns and beams that have no structural role.

The Amphitheatre in the Centre of Nîmes

The structure of the amphitheatre back in the centre of Nîmes was made using the same sort of constructional method – a concrete core, covered in stone. Here, though, in the city, the building was designed to impress, so it has columns modelled round its façades (*see* Fig. 16). As we saw at the temple, round the cella, these are pilasters – for visual, not structural effect. The raked seating inside the building is supported by concrete vaults, and arches are visible between the pilasters of the façade. The fullest development of this kind of building is in the centre of Rome itself,

at the Colosseum – a vast and complex building that had no equal anywhere.

The Colosseum

The Colosseum was built from 70CE, started by the emperor Vespasian (*see* Fig. 17). He took office as the fourth emperor in a particularly murderous year, and managed to inaugurate a period of stability where the empire was ruled by his family. The amphitheatre was known at the time as the Flavian Amphitheatre, because the family name was Flavius. Both Vespasian and his son had the name Titus Flavius Vespasianus, but on becoming emperor he changed it to Caesar Flavius Augustus, while his son became the emperor known as Titus. The amphitheatre was later called the Colosseum because of a huge statue – 30m tall – of

the emperor Nero that stood outside it. The area had been the site of the Golden House (Domus Aurea), one of Nero's palaces – estimates of its size put it at about 40 hectares (100 acres) and up – the size of a substantial country estate, which was an astonishing size for a property in central Rome.

Vespasian opened up the estate to the public and built the amphitheatre on the site of a decorative lake. The dwellings of ordinary free Romans were not good. They were cramped, piled high, and inclined to collapse. Many slaves who lived in larger houses had more secure roofs over their heads. The things that made life bearable were the entertainments such as chariot racing, fights to the death staged for an audience, and the lavish baths that gave people a taste of luxury. When Vespasian demolished Nero's Golden House and made the space part of the city again, that would have been welcome. The events staged in the Flavian Amphitheatre were absolutely thrilling. The statue was moved and adjusted to turn it into the sun god Sol.

The Colosseum survives as an impressive ruin – still an imposing presence in central Rome. In places its outer wall still stands to its full height with its stone cladding still in place, modelled with a version of the classical orders. The façade looks as if it has four storeys. Each storey has a row of columns, with an entablature above it as in a Greek temple,

but here the columns are only decorative – they are not doing the work of supporting the building. That work is being done by mass concrete, which makes an immensely solid building behind the façade. It is pierced by arched openings between one column and the next, continuing right round the building in an uninterrupted steady rhythm.

There was never anything like that in Greek architecture until the Roman influence was felt. In Roman architecture it is very much the usual pattern to find an arch flanked by columns. For example it is there in a very pure way in the triumphal arches that glorified the emperors' military successes. The Arch of Titus, in the Roman Forum, within sight of the Colosseum, for example, has an arch flanked by two Corinthian pilasters on each side of it. A sculpted panel within the arch shows the Roman soldiers bringing the treasures from the Temple of Jerusalem into Rome in triumph, and an inscription asserting that Titus and his father Vespasian were gods.

Back on the façade of the Colosseum there are Corinthian pilasters too, but only on one of the storeys. At ground level they are Tuscan – plain shafts without flutes. Then a storey higher they have Ionic capitals, and above that Corinthian. The topmost tier does not have any arches and the pilasters there are flat instead of half-round, but they again have Corinthian capitals. In the Colosseum's glory days there would have been masts at that level to support a canopy that was rigged up to shade at least some of the seats within. The stone footings for the masts are still in place.

The main space of the interior is an oval arena, open to the sky, and it is surrounded by steeply raked seating, supported on vaults that are immediately behind the façade, so from the outside one would have been able to catch glimpses of people moving about, making their way to their places. There are many stairs within and corridors beneath the vaults, which carefully segregated the audience. Coming from the street, there was a direct but carefully controlled way through to the innermost rows of seats. The cheaper or free seats for the plebs – the unexceptional people – were further away from the action in the arena high up, so they would have climbed stairs and walked through more of the vaulted spaces on the upper floors to reach them.

Beneath the floor of the arena there was a system of corridors or tunnels that were used to lead people or large wild animals to places where they could be released through trapdoors into the ring where they would be attacked or goaded into attacking either people or other animals. Battles were re-enacted. Gladiators fought to the death, and criminals were executed – sometimes by being torn apart by animals – or auctioned off as slaves.

The amphitheatre was inaugurated by Titus with games that went on for 100 days, and on one exceptional day Suetonius tells us that 5,000 animals were killed. He might have been exaggerating, but it gives an impression of the scale of the spectacle. Suetonius goes on to say (in the next sentence) that Titus was naturally kind-hearted, so he is describing the games as an act of generosity to the people of Rome from the emperor. It sounds appalling to me, but in the cinema today there is a large audience for actors pretending to be beaten up or shot, and computer games sometimes invite us to pretend to kill or be killed – so it is not as if the instincts have been exorcised from us with the passage of time.

Contrasting Greek and Roman Work

Looking back to the Parthenon, which represents the high point of an earlier tradition, there is a huge difference not only in the scale of the work, but also the character of the architecture. The Parthenon is finely adjusted, with its very slightly curved lines and the slight adjustment of spacing of the columns, the stretching of the metopes and the non-repeating ornament of the frieze and metope panels. The Colosseum, by contrast, is repetitive – its arcades encircle the building with a rhythm that makes no changes. Its organisation is brilliant, not only in the design, but in bringing the necessary materials to the site and getting the workforce to put them into the correct positions. It would be a challenge even for a modern builder with theodolites and lasers to set out the site, and tricky to work out the dimensions of the openings, to make them the same size all the way round an elliptical circumference.

If the Parthenon has the character of a finely judged sculpture, the Colosseum has the character of a well-calibrated machine. The arches and columns are repetitive and overwhelming, and if they could have been made by machine they would have been. Of course everything about the Colosseum is hand made, but all traces of individuality have been eradicated. It took eight years to build the Colosseum (72–80CE), but the conquest of Judea was under way – commemorated in the Arch of Titus – so there was a supply of Jewish slaves, and it is estimated that 60,000 of them worked on the building. These are not circumstances in which artistic creativity flourishes. The ethos of the workplace must have been to get the job done. The organisation was formidable and the achievement astonishing, but it is an achievement of discipline and coercion, power and wealth.

There is something similar at stake with the temples. Already centuries earlier in Athens, temple building had taken on an aspect of aggrandising the state. In Rome the imperial state became very much more powerful, and when it decided that a grand display was needed, it exceeded anything that had gone before. The temple always needed a sanctuary around it, for the altar, and in Athens this sanctuary was not always set apart from the rest of the city, as it was with the Acropolis. The Agora in Athens was at the heart of the city, and it was designated as a sanctuary. The Hephaisteion presided over it – the Temple of Hephaistos, the blacksmith or craftsman god. The Agora was originally no more than an open space, which became established as the place where people would meet – to do business, to make public speeches, to play games – and the old Roman Forum (the Forum Romanum) was initially just such a space. It was the hub of the city, not arranged in a geometrical way. One building after another was added to the collection, and the space got crowded. The Basilica Giulia came to dominate the space, but there the important part of the building was the inside.

The first of the forums created as a separate entity around the Forum Romanum was a precinct in front of the Temple of Venus Genetrix commissioned by Julius Caesar. It was dedicated in 46BCE as part of his triumph – celebrating not one, but four major military victories, including his campaigns in Gaul and Egypt.

The arrangement of the temple made the forum in front of the temple into a well-defined space, surrounded with a colonnade, so the external space has a strong architectural effect and it reads as if it is part of the temple, rather than just its setting in the city.

There is a similar arrangement of forms in the Egyptian temples that would have made a recent impression on the Consul (Julius Caesar) – a rectangular courtyard in front of the colonnaded temple. In Rome, though, the outside of the forum's walls are not conceived as an exterior – they merge with the rest of the city, and the portals are not placed on axis. One arrives by an irregular path and finds oneself in a well-defined open clearing in the city – the forum. The temple is placed on axis with it, and once there the formality takes over in quite a rigid way. This is quite different from the way the Greek temples – and the earlier Roman temples – were placed on their sites. The arrangement is easier to draw accurately on the page – straight lines parallel or at right-angles to one another – but more difficult to achieve on an irregular site, such as central Rome, famous for its hills, and where there were already other buildings around.

Fig. 18 Forum Romanum. The side vaults of the Basilica of Maxentius are visible on the left of the image. Its central space collapsed long ago, but was covered by a vault that was very like the one that survives from the Baths of Diocletian (*see* Fig. 20 below). The Arch of Titus is visible in the distance on the right, with the Colosseum rather lost beyond it. The Basilica Giulia would have been in the foreground to the right.

History of Ancient Rome Traced through Buildings

The Temple of Venus

Julius Caesar claimed that he was descended from Aeneas, a Trojan prince who came to Italy. The poet Virgil, who was writing at the time of Julius and Augustus Caesar, says that Aeneas was an ancestor of Romulus and Remus, also that his mother was Venus. Part of the rhetoric of the Temple of Venus Genetrix was to promote the claim that the Consul was descended from a god and ancient royalty. Venus Genetrix is Venus the Mother – the matriarch of the line of Caesar.

This divine status was embraced by his successors, the emperors, in a way that had not been part of Roman tradition before. It was a long-established part of Egyptian tradition, where the Pharaohs were thought of as divine, and where there were mammisi temples that commemorated and sacralised the divine conception of a member of a ruling family. Julius had a son with Cleopatra, Caesarion, who was brought up believing himself to have divine blood. The Temple of Venus was exactly a mammisi temple for Julius Caesar – laying claim to a divine line of descent, detailed in the relief sculptures and inscriptions in the forum's colonnade.

Julius was murdered by senators, who thought he was claiming too much power. They were hunted by Augustus, his successor, and defeated at the Battle of Philippi. The Forum Giulium here – the setting for the Temple of Venus – inaugurates a tradition of building that geometrically defined outdoor spaces in central Rome. The next one was the Forum Augustum, built by Augustus and dominated by the temple of Mars Ultor – Mars the avenger. It was conceived as a harmonious companion to the temple of Venus, and as a declaration of vengeance achieved.

With the deaths of the Consul's murderers, in 42BCE Augustus instructed the senate to acknowledge Julius as a god. In 27BCE Augustus became the first emperor, and after his death in 17BCE he also was declared a god.

The Temple of Mars Ultor

The senate normally met in the Curia on the old Forum Romanum, which was an important gathering place in the city, where crowds might form – though by the time of Augustus it was fiercely policed, especially when the senate was in session. The Forum of Augustus was by contrast a backwater – not exactly private, but especially when it was being used for senate business it must have had the character of a well-secured government building. There was a thick wall the height of the temple separating it from the fire risk of the housing immediately behind, and access to the forum was through a very few openings at the other end. The main approach was through the Forum of Caesar, crossing the space in front of the Temple of Venus. So unlike the Forum Romanum there would be no casual traffic passing through.

Augustus directed that the temple of Mars Ultor be used by the senate when it met to take decisions about war – under the watchful eye of the great marble statue of Mars (the god of war). There were eight 33m tall columns across the temple's façade, with Corinthian capitals, some of which survive. The capitals are themselves about 3m tall and are finely carved with rows of stylised acanthus leaves – there is nothing perfunctory about them. The whole project is grandly conceived and well made, the temple raised up on a storey-high podium, so the effect of the temple frontage in the confined space of the forum was impressive to the point of being overbearing, giving an impression of the empire's military power.

The interior of the building had columns with capitals that incorporated at the corners thunderbolt-carrying horses with outstretched wings (*see* Fig. 19). The capitals on the outside of the building are canonic – the authoritative Corinthian type – whereas those inside are more idiosyncratic, appropriate to this particular place. The thunderbolt capital is repeated within this interior, but it is not to be found in other buildings.

Fig. 19 Capital from the interior of the temple of Mars Ultor, Rome (consecrated 2BCE). The capital has winged horses instead of the usual volutes at the corners.

Augustus's Mausoleum

Augustus also commissioned a mausoleum, which became the dynastic tomb for the imperial family – including several emperors. There was an altar associated with it, the Ara Pacis – the altar of peace: it is miraculously well preserved, and is even more remarkable than the Pergamon altar. Its low-relief sculptures show animals – sheep and cows – being brought to sacrifice. A frieze shows ox skulls with garlands draped between them, which is a permanent version of a kind of decoration that must have been rehearsed in earlier altars. The ox skulls would have been real, from previous sacrifices, and garlands of real flowers would have been festive for the day. Here they have become permanent.

Trajan's Forum

The biggest of the imperial fora was commissioned by Trajan, who became emperor in 98CE and lived until 117CE – a hundred years after Augustus. Trajan expanded the empire with his conquests of Dacia (Romania) and Mesopotamia (Iraq), and it was under his reign that it was at its most extended – but these conquests were problematic and his successors had to cede territory. There were gold mines in Dacia and they helped to pay for Trajan's Forum – a vast complex that included a temple dedicated to Trajan after he had been made a god by his successor Hadrian, a huge basilica, enclosed open space, and libraries that made a courtyard with tiered colonnades around it.

In the courtyard is a decorated column (*see* Fig. 20). It is the best known of Trajan's building works, because it has survived. It stands 30m high, on a base with a dedicatory inscription that raises it 3m higher. Trajan's ashes were buried at the base of the column, and a statue of him stood on the top of it (now replaced by a late sixteenth-century statue of Saint Peter). The capital is Doric or Tuscan, but the shaft is neither plain nor fluted. It is sculpted with a finely modelled frieze that spirals its way up the whole height of the shaft. It has the rhythms of a comic strip and the seriousness of the Parthenon frieze, and tells the story of Trajan's Dacian campaigns, packed with incidents involving soldiers, horses, the River Danube and road-building through forests to get the army into position.

Fig. 20 *On the right* Trajan's column, Rome (107–113CE), with the huge neoclassical confection of the Victor Emmanuel monument in the background – commissioned to mark the unification of Italy (1885–1935).

Trajan's Market

Adjacent to this complex there was a much more utilitarian building – Trajan's Market – which belongs to the realm of everyday life and helped with the distribution of the food supply to the citizens. It was solidly built in brick with a concrete core and part of it still stands, near the column, as a reminder that Trajan's works addressed the citizens' everyday needs as well as his own glorification. Most of Trajan's buildings have disappeared from view, including the vast bathing complex that bore his name. Excavations find a fine mosaic here and there that can be identified as belonging to it, but they are scant traces of something that was important in the city in its day.

Thermae: The Bathing Complexes

The more impressive remains of thermae – the bathing complexes – are those commissioned by Diocletian and Caracalla. What becomes very clear in these buildings is that Roman architecture moved far beyond the inherited example of the Greeks and developed the classical tradition to make huge vaulted spaces. The traditional temples and the fora open to the sky were surrounded by columns or pilasters and were straightforward developments of the Greek architectural language, but the vaults were a Roman innovation. They developed from the arch, and the most straightforward type of vault is known as the barrel vault. It is in principle just an arch that has been thickened – extruded – or a series of arches built one behind the other. It is there in the triumphal arches: the underside of the arch becomes a vault, often divided into square boxes (coffering).

Barrel vaults can be seen in the surviving part of the Basilica of Maxentius that stands between the Forum of Augustus and the Forum Romanum (*see* Fig. 18). The form is geometrically easy to resolve. It could be built in blocks of stone without running into problems trying to cut the blocks to the correct shape – the tapering voussoirs of the arch can be laid out with a ruler and compasses, or at the scale of a building, with a stylus and stretched string.

The same cannot be said for the groin vault, which looks as if two barrel vaults are intersecting one another at right-angles. The two cylinders form a ridge where they intersect – a groin – and to make this with precision takes a much greater level of skill on the part of the stone cutters. It cannot be done straightforwardly in a single plane, but involves some projective geometry. Most Roman groin vaults avoid these problems of cutting stones to the correct shape (stereotomy) by constructing the vaults in concrete. The problem then becomes how to erect the timber formwork – itself quite a feat, but more manageable – so the concrete can be poured and set. Then the timber is removed. The surface could then be covered with thin sheets of marble or mosaic.

The engineering principle of the arch and the vault would have been rehearsed and developed in small buildings that are now lost. There are many rustic versions of the vault, including imprecise groin vaults, in the cellars of pre-industrial houses in European villages. Here the stones are not precisely shaped – they are usually field stones, not cut and quarried, but salvaged as rubble from farmland. The timber formwork would be set up, or maybe a mound of earth, and the stones put in place. Then the whole thing is made to work by being covered in mortar or concrete that fills in the irregular gaps between the unshaped stones and makes them support one another.

To make such a vault on the scale of a farmhouse is something that was within reach of ordinary rural builders, but to make it on the scale of the Baths of Diocletian demands a level of expertise and organisation that has always been rare, and for every society before the Romans it was impossible. The great groin vault from the Baths of Diocletian survives. It was built about 300CE and turned into a church by Michelangelo over a thousand years later (*see* Fig. 21).

What kind of a bath needs a vault on this scale? It is not a functional requirement for bathing in itself, and it is clear from the buildings that the public baths of imperial Rome came to be about much more than just bathing. The first emperor to open a grand bathing establishment was Titus, who in 81CE presented the public with access to a bathing complex (Thermae Titi) that remained popular for hundreds of years. The

Fig. 21 The vault of the Baths of Diocletian, Rome (300CE). It was reused and is now the vault of the church of Santa Maria degli Angeli e dei Martiri, designed by Michelangelo Buonarotti, 1563–64.

building's location and grandeur make one suspect that it was formerly part of Nero's Golden House that was at this site, and its presentation to the public is part of the same gesture as the building of the nearby Colosseum, begun by Titus's father Vespasian but completed and inaugurated by Titus in 80CE.

The baths escalated in size and complexity with subsequent benefactions, culminating in the Baths of Caracalla (216CE) and the Baths of Diocletian (inaugurated 305CE), by when the type had become established and a person who knew their way around one would not be lost in the others. The Baths of Caracalla used so much water that they had their own dedicated aqueduct to fill the bathing pools, irrigate the gardens and make the fountains dance. Some of the water was heated – for the hot room (caldarium) – where the walls and floor were heated from behind and beneath.

The Roman method for cleansing involved not only plunging into water, but also promoting perspiration to sweat the city's grime out of the body's pores. There was also an unheated open-air pool for cooling off. In addition to the bathing facilities there were libraries and places to relax in the extensive gardens. Some of the services would have had to be paid for – refreshments, sex-workers – but the idea was that the baths were accessible for a modest charge or none at all, so that any Roman citizen could feel that they could have a taste of imperial luxury. The setting was magnificent, with the spectacular vaults, floors covered in mosaic, and a veneer of classical decoration on the massive structural walls.

It was in the sites of the gardens of the various bathing establishments that the finest ancient marble sculptures were later found – the ones that are now accessible to us in contemporary museums, such as the Vatican's collection. They were real palaces for the people. They might have to go home to squalid cramped rooms in tenement blocks liable to collapse, but they could conduct their social lives in the most grandiose of settings. They lived the dream of being Roman.

The Pantheon

The best preserved of all the buildings of ancient Rome is the Pantheon, built under Hadrian and dedicated in 128CE (*see* Figs 22 and 23). It has lost the forum that was its original setting, and some of its ornament, but its great bronze doors are still in place, and the main structure is still there – and what a structure it is. The main space was the largest dome that had ever been built. The next one to come close was the dome of Hagia Sophia in Constantinople, which is in the next chapter. The first dome to be actually larger was built in Florence in the fifteenth century – 1,300 years later. The Pantheon's dome is made of concrete, cast with coffers, each of which had a gilded bronze rosette, so it was like an idealised geometric model of the heavens studded with stars.

As a temple it is extraordinary because its interior is so important. It might have had an external altar like the other temples, but the interior is so

Fig. 22 The Pantheon (125CE), exterior. The best preserved Roman temple, but not the standard type. The exterior reused columns from an earlier building.

Fig. 23 The Pantheon, interior, showing the coffered concrete vault.

impressively ornamented that it must surely have been a place for solemn ceremonies, even if the sacrifices were made outside. Maybe sacrifices were not made here at all, and there are doubts as to whether it was actually considered to be a temple when it was built. Its name – which seems to mean that it was dedicated to all the gods – was a popular nickname for the place, not its official name, and in Roman religion all the gods would not be in one place – some of them dwelt in far-flung places. One of the ways of helping along the siege of a foreign city was to find the names of the gods who dwelt there, and to start making sacrifices to them, to win them over to the Roman side of the battle. Worship could be quite a practical, transactional affair in those days.

There was an earlier building here, and its dedicatory inscription was reused, but we know not to believe it when it claims Agrippa as the benefactor. It was Hadrian who caused it to be rebuilt and redesigned after a fire. In an age of mass production and machine tools we can forget how significant was the effort that went into the production of buildings. The granite columns were quarried in Egypt and brought to Rome intact, each shaft a monolith (which contrasts with the Greek tradition of building up the columns of stone drums, which were finished in situ). They are imposing, and originally they sat at the top of a flight of steps (the surrounding ground level has been raised) and would have been quite overbearing.

However, the building design anticipated that they would be higher, and there is an awkward junction between the portico and the rest of the building, which is the height it needs to be to contain a perfect sphere – the upper half made real with the dome. It makes the columns look as if they were reused from an earlier building, and the fact that they were not remade to fit the building properly – even on a project of such prestige – shows how much trouble it took to make and bring them.

The building is so well preserved because it was turned into a church relatively early. This might have been possible because pagan sacrifices were not being made there, so there was no need to stop them. More crucially the building adapted very well into a church because its interior space was the important thing about it. The Roman Empire's official adoption of Christianity will be discussed in the next chapter.

The greatest engineering triumphs of the empire were the concrete structures that made it possible for the Romans to cover huge spaces with vaults that seemed to float above the activities that went on beneath them. The activities themselves could be stately and dignified, as in the basilicas, hedonistic, as in the baths, or utilitarian, as in Trajan's markets. Trajan himself remarked that many architects came to Rome from Greece – he was writing to the governor of Bithynia, east of Byzantium, who had asked for an architect to be sent from Rome, but Trajan thought he would do better to look more locally.

What Makes Roman Architecture Classical?

What makes Roman architecture classical is its continued use of the Greek orders, or variations of them. Sometimes, as in the portico of the Pantheon, the structure could be like the Greeks' use of columns supporting a heavy masonry entablature, but more often the structure was a concrete wall with decorative columns or pilasters and a facing of marble. The coloured and figured marbles delighted the Romans, and they were brought from the places where they could be quarried – not always close to Rome. They had the organisation and resources to make that happen. Often these facings have been lost, so the structures are exposed as brick-covered concrete.

An International Style

What makes Roman architecture particularly important in the story of classical architecture is that the Romans used the classical details in buildings throughout the empire, to give official buildings authority and dignity. This planted the idea of classical architecture on land all round the Mediterranean, and that stretched from the Atlantic and the North Sea to the Black Sea and did so two thousand years ago, so it has had time to be assimilated and naturalised as part of the culture of a great many places. There are regional inflections in the style, but it was well and truly internationalised by the Romans, so any citizen of the empire, or from lands that once belonged to it, can feel a sense of familiarity with classical forms.

Chapter Three

Byzantium

Early Christian Rome

Nowadays when we talk about the Byzantine style we normally mean the style of medieval Greece, but it is more complicated than that. Byzantium was a Greek city in the Roman Empire that flourished as a trading place where the land routes from east to west intersected with the north–south traffic of the sea. It was on the Bosporus, the natural strait that connects the eastern Mediterranean with the Black Sea, and the city levied tolls from the ships that went through. It prospered. Then in 324 the emperor Constantine (280–337 CE) adopted it as a new seat of imperial government, renaming it Constantinople. He had plenty of reasons for doing so. Rome had grown beyond the capacity of its infrastructures, which were not up to the job of keeping its sanitation in good order – despite the monumental baths and sewers – fire and plague were continuing problems, and the empire's greatest wealth and territories were now well to the east.

Constantine's mother Eleni (Helen) was Greek and converted to Christianity, which Constantine in 313 decreed was an official religion of the Roman Empire. He too adopted Christianity, but was baptised only late in his life. Eleni searched the Holy Land for relics of Christ's life, and believed she found many of them, including the True Cross and the Crown of Thorns. It was under her influence that buildings were erected around Christ's tomb and at Golgotha – the site of Christ's crucifixion and his tomb.

Constantine defeated Maxentius to become emperor, and he completed the monumental basilica that Maxentius had begun to build in Rome (*see* Chapter 2). Constantine's other commissions in Rome included a mausoleum – now partially collapsed – for his mother, and another for his daughter Constantina, which has become a church dedicated to Santa Costanza (Figs 24 and 25). The church is the major new building type to take shape at this moment, as Christian worship became something that could be done openly.

The earliest places for Christian worship were hidden: private houses where people would meet, or the underground catacombs – former mine workings – where there were secret burials and shrines. One of these catacombs carries the name of Saint Agnes (who was supposed to be buried there) and

Fig. 24 Santa Costanza, Rome (350 CE), exterior.

lies beneath Constantina's mausoleum, which was envisaged as part of a huge basilica that would have incorporated other mausolea. These two forms – the cylindrical mausoleum and the basilica with a tall central space flanked by lower aisles – would become the regular recognised forms of churches.

Worship in Church: Interior Space

Worship in church was very different from worship at a pagan temple. A temple was there principally to house the cult statue of a god, and the festivals took place mainly outside the temple building, but within its sanctuary. The altar would be used to sacrifice animals, which would not be brought into the temple. By contrast the 'altar' in a Christian church is within the building, and in fact it is not an altar at all in the sense of it being a place to kill animals – as it had been in the Greek and Roman traditions and in the Jewish temple at Jerusalem. The Christian ceremony used bread and wine, evoking Jesus' last supper with his disciples, so the altar becomes a table and the congregation witnesses and participates in the supper as

a reminder of Jesus's sacrifice. The congregation is indoors in the room with the table.

The basilica was adopted as the type of large internal space that could accommodate this form of worship. Its cultural overtones were appropriate. The 'royal presence chamber' (the Greek word for royal is *basilikos*) had become a place presided over by an image of the deified emperor, and now transformed into the house of God. It was used when large numbers of people would assemble.

The circular form of church was used when echoes of the mausoleum were appropriate, often when the body of a saint was a focus of attention – a martyrium.

The Church of the Holy Sepulchre

The two forms were used together in Jerusalem, where by Constantine's decree at Golgotha a temple that Hadrian had dedicated to Aphrodite was demolished. Christ's tomb, the site of his resurrection, was identified. It had been cut into the rock of a hill, which was substantially remodelled by Constantine's builders, to leave the tomb like an isolated tooth sticking

up from a plateau. A mausoleum-form church was constructed around it – a mausoleum to house an absent body – the church of the Holy Sepulchre (Fig. 26). Then across a courtyard there was a basilica, aligned with the tomb. The original building was demolished and there have been attacks and upgradings over the centuries, but the tomb survives, and excavations have established the lines of Constantine's buildings.

Constantine's Basilicas in Rome

In Rome, Constantine transformed the fortunes of the Church by giving it important buildings, and the estates that would enable it to support them in perpetuity. The Lateran family's lands had been forfeited to Constantine and he made them over to the Church, which established its administrative headquarters and a huge basilica outside the historic centre of Rome, even though the centre was already congested with monumental buildings that Constantine did nothing to disturb. He accepted and encouraged Christianity, but did not want to abolish paganism, which would have alienated the traditional (and still powerful) ruling class. The Lateran Basilica

and the papal palace attached to it remained the seat of Church government until the fourteenth century, when it moved to the papal palace in Avignon, France (Fig. 27).

Constantine also ordered the construction of a basilica incorporating the tomb of St Peter – Christ's senior apostle. According to tradition he had been crucified upside down at a chariot-racing stadium, the Circus of Nero, at a time when Nero was killing Christians. The grounds of the circus and its gardens therefore became the site for the basilica, which remained in place for over a thousand years (until the sixteenth century). Most of its columns followed the established Roman Corinthian pattern, but Constantine sent from Greece a set of twelve twisted columns that he believed had come from Solomon's long-demolished temple in Jerusalem. In Rome they stood in a row across the east end of the basilica, in front of the apse that housed St Peter's tomb. Eight of them survive, in the upper part of the piers under Michelangelo's dome in the modern church (Fig. 28).

They were idiosyncratic, but given their prominence and provenance they had authority (even if they were not known to Solomon, they were a gift from Constantine). Any Roman who knew the grand basilicas around the city's forums would have found the

Fig. 27 Lateran basilica, Rome (consecrated 324CE). One of Constantine's churches, and the original seat of the papacy.

Fig. 28 Saint Peter's basilica, Rome. The illustration shows the church as it is today, rebuilt by Michelangelo and others (*see* Chapters 5 and 6). The prominent baldacchino with dark, twisted columns is by Bernini (*see* Chapter 6). It covers the high altar, directly beneath Michelangelo's dome. In between the two columns of the baldacchino on the left there is an arrangement with two twisted columns at high level. They are two of the columns that were given to the original basilica by Constantine.

new churches completely familiar. Their architecture spoke of continuity with the established order. It very deliberately did not look like a revolution.

The Church of the Holy Apostles, Constantinople

In Constantinople the first great church that Constantine commissioned was the Church of the Holy Apostles. It was still unfinished at Constantine's death, but he was buried there alongside the relics of as many apostles as they could find. It had a central dome and four equal wings, which made it a new departure from the fully cylindrical mausoleum. Eusebius (263–339) described the building, and it sounds as if it was classical in the expected Roman style, covered in coloured marble, with brass roof tiles (the Pantheon had gilded bronze roof tiles in Constantine's day, but they were at some point removed and brought to Constantinople) – but then Eusebius makes it clear that there is plenty of gilding in the architectural ornament, and the whole dome was covered with decorative swirls of gilded brass – so it sounds as if the exterior work was more lavishly ornamental than anything in Rome itself.

The Byzantine Empire

Rome's eminence as a seat of power was beginning to slide. Before long the empire was divided into a western Latin-speaking half and an eastern Greek-speaking half. The west was governed from Rome and then from Ravenna (from 402). Rome fell to Goths and Germans in 475 and in effect the western Roman empire ceased at that point to be politically significant. The eastern empire continued – not without its own problems – surviving until 1453 when Constantinople was invaded by the Turks. So the rule from Constantinople lasted for a thousand years – longer than there had been a Roman empire in the west.

We call the eastern empire Byzantine, but the people who ruled it thought of themselves as Roman. They continued to use Roman building methods and knowledge. The Roman traditions were still alive there. The imperial palace had mosaic floors – some of which survive in fragments – such as Roman villas, and of course the imperial baths in Rome. Alongside it there was the Hippodrome, where horses and chariots raced, as they did in Rome. Constantinople was 'the new Rome', but the language was Greek, and it was the capital of the Greek-speaking world. Anything medieval and Greek is now called Byzantine, and Constantinople was the capital of the medieval Greek world.

Byzantine Churches

Saint Polyeuktos

In 524 a spectacular new church was begun, under the patronage of Anicia Juliana (462–528). She was an imperial princess, prominent because of her great wealth and her aristocratic pedigree – descended from western emperors and with a sense of her family's dynastic right to the imperial throne, but unrelated to the then emperor, Justin (450–527) who had no such lineage. He had come up through the ranks in the army and outmanoeuvred his rivals, but was already seventy when he came to the throne. The building of the church, Saint Polyeuktos, was designed to emphasise Anicia Juliana's nobility and splendour and to enhance her family's claims on the throne when the aged emperor left it.

It was the largest church in the city, domed like the church of the Holy Apostles, but here sitting on a squared basilica. The transition between the circle of the dome and the square that supported it was managed into elegant pendentives – which is to say that, seen from the interior, there was a curved triangular surface, part of a hollow sphere, between the dome and the square of the walls beneath it. There was a huge mass of masonry behind this surface, giving the dome very adequate support, but which could not be seen from the interior, so the dome would have seemed almost to float. It was the most sophisticated engineering the city had seen.

The space of the church was impressive, but what really made it dazzle was its rich decoration. The church was destroyed, but fragments of its masonry have been salvaged or carried off as plunder. For example, some of its columns stand outside San Marco in Venice (*see* Fig. 29). The capitals of its columns were not the standard Corinthian type, but clearly owed something to it. They were elaborated with leaves, flowers and insignia, as were the columns' shafts, so the classical language is here being developed into something more decorative than ever, and the sense of the solidity of the forms is less important than the elaboration of the surfaces. Spread peacocks' tails decorated the semi-circular top part of niches around the central space, and a frieze inscribed with texts from Solomon's psalms established a claim for the building to be seen in the tradition of Solomon's temple in Jerusalem (described in the biblical *Book of Kings*). The expectation was that the church would be further embellished by the future emperors from Anicia Juliana's family, but that was not how it worked out.

The church that was tied most closely to the impartial court came to be known as Hagia Sophia. The original basilica was built by Constantine's successor, Constantius, and it was like the other large Roman basilicas. Soon after the dedication of Saint Polyeuktos the emperor Justin died, and he was

Fig. 29 These two columns outside San Marco in Venice came from the church of Saint Polyeuktos in Constantinople (now Istanbul). They date from 525CE, but were brought to Venice as trophies in the thirteenth century.

succeeded not by anyone from Anicia Juliana's family, but by Justinian, a nephew of Justin.

The Basilica of Hagia Sophia

The old basilica of Hagia Sophia was badly damaged by fire in riots in 532, and Justinian completely rebuilt it as an edifice of unparalleled magnificence, completely outdoing every other church in Christendom (*see* Fig. 30). It is recognisably the same pattern of church as Saint Polyeuktos, with a central dome with pendentives covering an interior that is arranged like a basilica, with side aisles and galleries. The scale is larger. The central dome is almost as large as that of the Pantheon, but its effect is even more astonishing, because it is supported by ribs that allow a ring of windows to run round the base of the dome, enhancing the effect of it seeming to float weightlessly over the throngs below.

The columns in the building are recognisably classical in style, but the idea of the Corinthian is elaborated with stones that are sometimes so deeply undercut that the decorative work looks like a lace cover that is floating round the capital. Others have inlaid coloured stones, and drilled decoration. The sense of modelling is quite different from the capitals of the Greek pagan temples, which look as though they were conceived by sculptors who modelled with a fully three-dimensional sense of form. By contrast the sculptors of Constantinople tended to prefer low-relief panels, and the carving of capitals turned into ever-more-elaborate treatments of the surface.

The surfaces of the walls and vaults also became very important. They were covered in decorative marbles or mosaics, and the mosaics were a place for figurative Christian imagery – images of saints, Christ, the Virgin Mary and angels, mixed with court figures and donors. At Hagia Sophia the figures were set against gold mosaic backgrounds, and the gold was the dominant colour of the interior. From the central part of the building few windows are visible, but the gold mosaics reflected light around the interior. It was not clear where the light was coming from, and it seemed to be generated by the space itself. The descriptions of miracles associated with the building began before it was completed, and the very fact that it did not collapse was seen as a miracle.

The Church of Saints Sergius and Bacchus

At the same time as this building was under construction, the same architects put up another, which has similar geometry and could have been a full-dress experiment to alert them to potential problems with the larger building. It was the church of Saints Sergius and Bacchus, and the building survives (with adjustments) as a mosque. The architects were Anthemios of Tralles (474–534) and Isidore of Miletus (442–537), who were mathematicians by training (geometers) but they must have had some prior experience of building work. They engaged with the tradition of Roman engineering that had produced great vaulted structures in Rome, and in Hagia Sophia it seems to be used with great confidence – domes and half-domes supporting and balancing one another.

It is astonishing that the structure has survived. There was some damage after an earthquake in 558, when the central dome collapsed. It was rebuilt with more curvature than before, making it a little steeper and taller, and more stable. The slight irregularity in the form of the surviving structure makes it seem that it is absolutely at the edge of what could be achieved – but it was built, and it is still there (Fig. 30). When Justinian first set foot in the great space he is supposed to have said 'Solomon, I have outdone thee!'. The building was certainly seen in the tradition of great buildings that included both Solomon's temple and the more recent Solomon-evoking building for Anicia Juliana.

The State's Connection with the Church

It was in this place until 1453 that the emperor acted out the state's close connection with the

Fig. 30 Isidorus of Miletus and Anthemios of Tralles, Hagia Sophia, Constantinople (Istanbul) (consecrated 537CE). Originally this was the church of the Byzantine emperors, but after 1453 it was turned into a mosque.

church, in elaborate rituals witnessed by the court and the reverent public. Under Justinian the empire remained powerful, and it was under his leadership that Italy was reclaimed for the empire. At Ravenna there are numerous church buildings with spectacular mosaics that were executed by craftsmen from Constantinople. They include portraits of Justinian and the empress Theodora, and give us an idea of the intensity of colour that the mosaics at Hagia Sophia would once have had.

Christian imagery in general has had a more troubled time of it in Constantinople, as it was either destroyed or plastered over after the Turkish conquest brought Islam and a prohibition against images of religious figures. Images in the west – such as those in Ravenna and the area that became modern Greece – have survived more straightforwardly. Hagia Sophia was overwhelmingly the greatest church in the greatest city of the empire, and there was nothing else like it. Nor did there need to be. There was only one emperor, and the church continued to be there, along with the great palace and the Hippodrome, all demonstrating the continuity with Rome and classical antiquity, even while the style of the art and architecture gradually changed.

Other Byzantine Church Buildings

The church buildings that are familiar from the rest of the empire are relatively small and in engineering term unambitious, even when they are finely built and decorated. For example there is a concentration of good churches at Mystras, which was the administrative capital of the Peleponnese in the middle ages, not far from Sparta. Constantine Palaeologos, the last Byzantine emperor, was living here when he was called to Constantinople to assume his office.

The churches are of modest size, their walls covered with paintings showing religious imagery. Architecturally it is the interior surfaces that are important, because they carry the paintings. Classical ornament is not forgotten, but it is confined to cornices and the capitals of piers that merge into the walls, rather than being fully developed columns. These are much more characteristic of the general run of Byzantine buildings (Fig. 31).

The great monuments of Constantinople were the exception, and they date from the relatively early days of the eastern empire, so sometimes they are described as 'Late Roman'. However, they did not go away. Through the long life of the empire they were

Fig. 31 Saint Demetrios' church at Mystras (late thirteenth century).

very much present and an influence on architectural thinking. Their silhouettes are still present in the modern city of Istanbul, not only in the surviving Byzantine buildings, but also in the mosques that were built to emulate and outdo them from the sixteenth century onwards.

The Schism between the Eastern and Western Churches

Constantinople became a byword for riches and sophistication across the medieval world. The churches held many holy relics, and it was an important centre for Christianity. However, in 1054 there was a recognised schism that formalised the differences in teaching that had developed between the eastern and western churches, so the Orthodox Patriarch in Constantinople and the Catholic Pope in Rome guided the faith along different lines. At times Venice was part of the Byzantine empire, albeit with some detachment. The cathedral of San Marco in Venice gives the best idea that survives of the splendour of a Byzantine church of the highest rank.

Venice made a definitive break with Constantinople in 1171 with a declaration of war, and then in 1204

with the Fourth Crusade the Venetians were among those who sacked Constantinople and embellished Venice with the columns and statues in the Piazzetta San Marco, as well as spolia from Saint Polyeuktos and elsewhere. These were built into the church's walls, and the Roman cast-copper statues of horses that had been at the Hippodrome now stand above the Venice church's central doorway (*see* Fig. 32).

Like Hagia Sophia, San Marco was closely linked with the ruler of the place. The Doge of Venice was elected – it was not an inherited position. The Venetian empire remained intact until Napoleon's arrival in 1797, when the last doge abdicated. At that point San Marco became Venice's cathedral. Until then the bishop and patriarch of Venice had their establishments elsewhere in the city, while San Marco accumulated the city's treasures, such as the Pala d'Oro, the gold, gem-studded panel set with Byzantine enamel images of saints that is set on the high altar. The five domes on pendentives that cover the main spaces have their mosaics with gold backgrounds still in place.

There are times when it can seem that Byzantine churches are so preoccupied with the symbolism of the interior and its images that the exterior has just been left to take care of itself. San Marco shows how, with the accretion of ornament and the desire

Fig. 32 San Marco, Venice (consecrated 1094). This is a Byzantine building, but built outside the Byzantine Empire, as the chapel for the doge of Venice. The horses above the entrance are Roman treasures brought as trophies from Constantinople (*see* Fig. 29).

to put on a good show for an important civic space, the interior's splendour can be translated to the outside. It would have been this kind of enrichment that Anicia Juliana might have anticipated for her temple in Constantinople, but the churches there were depleted savagely in 1204 by the Crusaders, and again after 1453 when many of them were turned into mosques.

The Transformation of Byzantine Style

Vaults and Domes

Byzantine style grew out of classical architecture and became something that was quite different from the ancient Greek temples in which it originated, transformed by way of the great vaults that were developed at Rome. It went through a further transformation at the hands of the Ottoman Turks, who were installed at Constantinople from 1453. It is remarkable that instead of plundering the city for its treasures and carrying them away, they adopted the city as their own capital, calling it Istanbul (which means 'the city'). The Christian Greek-speaking population dispersed, especially the educated classes, who took their knowledge of the Roman tradition of classical texts with them when they resettled.

In 1453 no great vaults had been built at Constantinople for hundreds of years. The technical expertise for constructing them had died out and there was a new civilisation in charge, so any lines of continuity had been broken. Hagia Sophia became a great mosque, but it was an ancient building, and in the sixteenth century the Sultan Suleyman the Magnificent decided it should be possible for his builders to manage something equally impressive. The story is that his first architect told him that it couldn't be done, and he was executed, so when Sinan was appointed as the imperial architect he was highly motivated to find a way to succeed. He oversaw the design and construction of the Suleyman Mosque, on the highest part of the city's land, where it still holds a dominant position in the city's skyline (Fig. 33).

It has been joined by other Ottoman-era domes, including that of the Sultanahmet Mosque, which is aligned with Hagia Sophia and matches its bulk and general configuration. It dates from the early seventeenth century (it was opened in 1616).

The engineering in these buildings is so accomplished that it looks effortless, and a similar sense of a huge volume of interior space was achieved without the great masses of masonry that are apparent at Hagia Sophia. These structures seem lighter and more permeable, and they are decorated in a much lighter way, with geometric designs and sacred texts. They have slender pointed towers around them, minarets, from which people are called to prayer, and these enhance the distant views and give the monuments a more emphatic presence. Where Western cities are traditionally anchored visually by the soaring spire of a cathedral, the profile of Istanbul is punctuated by domes, which mark out the great architectural achievements of two empires that both made this place their home.

Fig. 33 Mimar Sinan, Suleymaniye Mosque, Istanbul (1550–1557).

Chapter Four

Romanesque

After the Roman Empire

Constantine was in Eboracum in Britannia (now York in the north of England) with his father the emperor Constantius, when Constantius died. Two hundred years later Rome had fallen, and Roman administration of that part of the world had completely withdrawn. The Romans left buildings behind, but the indigenous population left them abandoned, having no use for them, and moved out of the towns back to the roundhouses that had sustained them before the Romans had arrived.

Other parts of the former empire have different histories. The Germanic tribes had always resisted being co-opted into the ancient empire. In France and Italy there were more monumental structures left behind, and some of them continued to be used. Without the organisation and concentrations of power, the buildings that were constructed tended to be modest – the kind of thing that local communities might be expected to build for themselves in an agricultural economy – of course using local materials, and meeting local practical and spiritual needs. In architectural history terms this makes it a 'dark age' because the buildings have mostly disappeared without trace, so it is difficult to be impressed by them. There are enough fine artefacts around – impressive jewellery, illuminated manuscripts – to show that there was cultural activity of a high order, but it was not directed into monumental stone buildings.

The example of the Romans stimulated attempts to emulate their achievements. In the place we call Aachen or Aix-la-Chapelle, in 795–803 a chapel appeared, now known as the Palatine Chapel, based on the church of San Vitale at Ravenna, which was built 538–547 – less than two hundred years earlier,

Fig. 34 Odo of Metz, Palatine Chapel, Aachen (Aix la Chapelle) (consecrated 804CE).

Fig. 35 Detail of mosaic at the Palatine chapel, Aachen.

but with clear imperial Roman patronage from the east. The chapel at Aachen (*see* Figs 34 and 35) was built for Charles, king of the Franks – Charles the Great, or Charlemagne (748–814). His court brought together people from across Europe, and on Christmas Day 800 the Pope crowned him Emperor of the Romans in Constantine's basilica of Saint Peter in Rome. At his court in Aachen he demonstrated in architecture his links with the institutions of the then-current Roman empire by replicating a building from Ravenna that would now be called Byzantine in style; however, Charlemagne would have thought of it as Roman, or we might think 'classical' – but the word was not used in that way at that time.

The size and shape of the building was close to that of San Vitale, its interior was covered in mosaics, and spolia from ruins in Rome and Ravenna was incorporated in the walls. The vault of the dome over the central space is not as large as in some of the grand imperial Roman structures, but compares with those of regionally important Byzantine churches (not with Hagia Sophia). It could be seen as continuing the Byzantine tradition of church building, but it is in a different part of the world – northern Europe – and it was co-opted by the Holy Roman Emperors who ruled German-speaking Europe and sometimes much more from the tenth century. They were crowned in the Palatine Chapel until the sixteenth century.

Reviving the Vault

The Monastery of Saint Philibert

At Tournus in Burgundy in about 1000 at the monastery of Saint Philibert, it was decided to build a bigger church and to cover it with a masonry vault. It is not clear where this idea came from. There are Roman ruins in the region, but nothing that stands has a vaulted structure, so perhaps people had heard about vaults in Rome, or someone in the community had travelled there and tried to explain to the masons what he had seen.

Whatever the circumstances, the results were unique and have the appearance of experimentation. This is not continuous with any Roman tradition, but is an attempt to revive a Roman practice by people who had not been trained in the Roman masons' ways of thinking and doing things. For example, in the lower side aisles the arches are not perfectly formed. Had they been built by expert Romans they would look regular and routine, but here they look as if they were a struggle to control, and as if the imperfections were outweighed by the success of building an arch

that would support itself – and which is still standing now, more than a thousand years later.

The nave is spanned by arches, which of course are larger, and seem to have been made with more assurance. Then above the arches a barrel vault was formed that spanned between one arch and the next – so looking down the nave of the church one sees the arches going across, one after another, each one with a section of wall above it that supports the springing of the barrel vault. If we go into the nave and look sideways, we can see the semi-circle of the vault reaching the side wall, and a window high up in that side wall (*see* Fig. 36).

The local vernacular tradition in the region produced many small-scale vaults under domestic buildings, using uncut stones from the fields and lots of mortar to hold everything together, instead of the careful shaping of stones that is characteristic of high-status masonry. So the masons would have understood the principle of a small, simple vault. Here at Saint Philibert's it is executed with much greater precision, with shaped stones. In the aisles, groin vaults are used, so that configuration was known to the masons, and later churches would have the

Fig. 36 Saint Philibert, Tournus (c.1000CE). The church belonged to an abbey that was founded in 875. The vaults shown here were probably built in the eleventh century.

Fig. 37 Roman city gate, known as the Porte d'Arroux, Autun (15BCE).

confidence to use them to cover larger spaces – as had the Romans.

Cathedral of Saint-Lazare, Autun

One sees at Autun (87km from Tournus) a strong link between the local Roman ruins and the architecture of the cathedral. The settlement was founded as an administrative capital by the Romans, who called the place Augustudunum, and it became – by the standards of the time – a large city. The remains of the Roman theatre are still to be seen there, and two city gates, each of which has a row of small arches running along above two much larger arches through which traffic once passed (Fig. 37). This arrangement is repeated in the cathedral, which was built in the twelfth century (1120–46) (*see* Fig. 38). The nave's arcades match those in the gates, but at a larger scale.

The scale is suggested by a ruined Roman temple, which is fancifully called the Temple of Janus. Two concrete walls of its cella survive, with small openings high in the wall above larger openings below. It is as

Fig. 38 Cathedral of Saint-Lazare, Autun (1120–46).

if the twelfth-century cathedral buildings, feeling a duty to rival the Romans, took the height of one monument and the decorative detail of the other to make their new basilica. The cathedral also has a remarkable vault, a simple barrel vault that spans the width of the nave and runs the whole length of it.

This is unusual for two reasons. One is that the vault is pointed, which is uncommon in a barrel vault. The other is that being a simple tube of a vault, there are no windows high up above the springing of the vault so it is not illuminated at a high level, and this makes it feel very gloomy and ponderous. The pattern of vaulting that came to be used in the later twelfth-century churches, such as at Vézelay (*see* Fig. 39), used groin vaults, which in effect take the semi-cylinder of the vault running along the nave, and

make it intersect with semi-cylinders going across it at right-angles. It is therefore possible to introduce high-level windows so the vaults are lit – as at Tournus, but more elegantly – and this gives them a more gracious and imposing presence, much closer to the precedents to be found in imperial Rome, which may not have been known to the medieval builders.

As at Constantinople, the classical base for the architectural thinking is apparent, but there are also departures from it. There are good copies of Corinthian capitals to be found here and there in Romanesque churches (*see* Fig. 40), but the characteristic capitals from them are elaborated with figures worked into them, acting out scenes from the Bible or from everyday life. These pictorial capitals, along with the vaults, developed into the Gothic style

Fig. 39 Basilica Sainte Madeleine, Vézelay (1120–50).

Fig. 40 Twelfth-century Corinthian capital at Vézelay.

that became the norm for medieval church architecture, taking the buildings to new heights and sometimes with extraordinary delicacy as the tradition of masonry became ingrained and developed with continuous learning across the centuries.

This tradition begins in the Romanesque and branches out from there. The Gothic is normally seen as having a distinct set of values and aesthetic concerns that separate it from Classicism, but it grows out of the Romanesque, which grows out of the Roman, and is part of the story of bifurcation

and proliferation that characterises more than one tendency in some of the classical traditions. Once the pattern of the Romanesque church was established – with regional variations – the masons looked at recent buildings and tried to outdo them. The soaring spires and delicate tracery of the Gothic have no precedent in classical architecture, but the Gothic cathedrals would not have developed the way they did without the generative patterns and the idea of stone vaults that came from earlier masons' desire to find a way to do what the Romans had done.

Continuity in Florence

The Church of San Miniato al Monte

At Florence the church of San Miniato al Monte was constructed from about 1018 (*see* Fig. 41). The upper part of its façade was put in place during the twelfth century, and the use of strongly contrasted marbles that pattern the façade gives it a brilliance that enables it to be seen very clearly from central Florence – looking out across the river it can be seen on its hill, gleaming a kilometre or so away.

The church is a basilica, but with a more complex spatial arrangement than one would anticipate. The level of the main floor of the nave is about half way between that of the crypt and that of the choir, and both of them are quite open to the nave. The apse behind and above the choir is decorated with mosaic that could be Byzantine – Christ Pantokrator on a gold background. The columns supporting the arches that march down the nave are salvaged Roman columns, and the intricately cut contrasting stones were certainly understood as a Roman way to finish a building. Most of the monastery is finished with plain masonry – a mixture of brick and stone – but the façade of the church was given special treatment that brings the decorative scheme of the interior to the outside of the building.

There are nine arches along the length of the nave, divided into three bays of three arches each. A large arch spans across the nave to mark out these bays. Each of them is decorated with the contrasting stone surface, like the exterior. These transverse arches give the impression of being in a vaulted space, but in fact heavy timber trusses can be seen up above, doing the work of supporting the roof – so the transverse arches are not structural, but decorative.

Fig. 41 San Miniato al Monte, Florence (1013–18).

The Cathedral in Florence

The baptistery at the cathedral in Florence is in a similar style (*see* Fig. 42). It looks Byzantine. The building is octagonal and its walls are faced in marble – patterned like the church of San Miniato up the hill. The space is covered by a dome of uncertain date that was decorated between 1225 and 1330 with gold-background mosaics. The images' designs were by artists from Florence, but they were turned into mosaics and applied by craftsmen who came from further east – Venice or Constantinople – so this again is in the established style of the Roman empire, and Giovanni Villani, writing in about 1300, believed it to be a Roman building that the craftsmen were decorating.

The Rib Vault: A Novel Way of Building

In the north of Europe the round-arch style of the Romanesque was superseded by the pointed-arch style that we now call Gothic – but that oversimplifies the story. What made the Gothic vaults possible was a novel way of building that was developed at Durham Cathedral (Fig. 43). The rib vault that is found there made it possible to build using very much less timber supporting framework while the vault was under construction.

The rib vault became the characteristic Gothic vault during the thirteenth to fifteenth centuries (and in later revivals). It is in place from 1093 in the aisles at Durham Cathedral, which is a Romanesque building with a particularly monumental character. It introduced some pointed arches, which are more characteristic of Gothic work, but not unknown in the Romanesque (for example at Autun in the cathedral's vault, and in the nave arcade of the great abbey at Cluny). At Durham they derive from the geometry of the vault that made the diagonal ribs true semi-circular arches, so the arches that go directly across the nave end up pointed. Earlier vaults, Roman

Fig. 42 Baptistery of Saint John, Florence (1059–1128).

Fig. 43 Saint Cuthbert's Cathedral, Durham (vaults c.1133).

and Romanesque alike, were groin vaults, which do not have arches expressed along their diagonal lines, but just a fold where the curvatures of two cylinders intersect.

The Cathedral Windows

The cathedral at Florence used the rib vaults and pointed arches, but did not follow the northern enthusiasm for making stained glass take over the walls. There are no buttresses evident here, especially not the flying buttresses that became such a powerful part of the architecture, for example at Bourges. At Florence the cathedral windows follow the established Romanesque pattern (Fig. 44). They are relatively small openings in the heavy walls, some of them in the aisles, while others, that are smaller, are higher up in the clerestory directly illuminating the nave. The building is far from dark. The Gothic idea of increasing the size of windows was not to give more light in the interior, but to dissolve the envelope of the building in the dazzling darkness of stained glass. No buildings in Florence accepted that ideal – rather, they continued with a sober classical monumentality.

The Cathedral Dome

The most celebrated part of the cathedral is its dome, which is huge and anchors the idea of the centre of the city of Florence when it is seen from the hills around (*see* Fig. 45). It is a spectacular technical achievement as well as being an imposing presence. The walls that support it were laid out to the design of Arnolfo di Cambio (1240–1300). He came to Florence in 1295, and he must have had the idea that there would be a huge dome over the cathedral's principal space, because the walls were arranged to make that space.

Fig. 44 Dome of the cathedral of Santa Maria del Fiore, Florence (1420–36).

Fig. 45 The city of Florence with the cathedral's dome clearly visible.

Its general pattern is like other thirteenth-century cathedrals in the region, such as Siena, in being laid out as a basilica with transepts, and with a dome over the crossing.

At Siena the dome was completed in 1264, and the cathedral building is clearly Romanesque throughout, with its forceful polychromy, round arches and classical capitals. This is true even in the huge extension that was planned in the fourteenth century, but abandoned when the city's population was reduced by plague. At Siena the dome is relatively small and makes a lantern that in principle brings light down into the heart of the cathedral, but actually it is so high up that very little of the light reaches the floor. Its effect is to lift the eyes up to the bright space high up in the vaulting.

At Florence by contrast the dome is huge. The cathedral's transepts are short – they have become semi-octagonal groups of chapels with a semi-dome over the space between them and the large central dome – a little like the configuration at Hagia Sophia, but here the space is octagonal rather than square, and the domes retain the facets of an octagon, so there is no need to make further adjustment between the dome and its base (no need for pendentives). The arches in these vaults and in the main dome itself are all slightly pointed, which is noteworthy because it shows that it was not such a high priority to follow the Romans.

The main dome is the work of Filippo Brunelleschi (1377–1446), and construction began in 1420. It was the first dome to be larger than the Pantheon's – which had been built 1,300 years earlier – so it was a breathtaking achievement. It is no less astonishing that the stage was set so much earlier. Arnolfo of Cambio's design for the building required this achievement. The lower parts of the building anticipated that it would be done, but no one knew how it could be done. If Arnolfo had had any idea how it could be done, that idea died with him. For over a hundred years generations of Florentines lived and died while their cathedral's principal space

remained unroofed, which was inconvenient and embarrassing. It seemed that the Florentines had been over-ambitious and had over-reached themselves, starting a project they could not complete. There was more at stake than a personal reputation: the city's prestige was in question.

When we hear about Brunelleschi in recent times he is presented as a pivotal figure who more or less invented the Renaissance – the rebirth of ancient Roman culture. This is partly because of the account that Vasari (1511–74) gives of Brunelleschi's life, which has Brunelleschi visiting Rome to study the ruins there for some years before returning to Florence with the idea of building the cathedral's dome. We do know that Brunelleschi visited Rome after the construction of the dome, but Vasari's story is unsupported by evidence. Vasari is now best remembered as the author of his *Lives* of Florentine artists, but he was also the artist who was commissioned to paint the underside of the dome.

The principal evidence for Brunelleschi's way of thinking is the dome itself, which is not built in a Roman way, and is not a Roman shape. It does reflect the shape of the cathedral's baptistery, which Brunelleschi saw as a Roman building, but not the shape of anything in Rome itself. The dome of the Pantheon is in concrete, built with timber shuttering to make its coffers. Once the concrete had set, the shuttering could be removed.

Brunelleschi's dome is in brick. It was made without being supported by temporary scaffolding from beneath during its construction, but by using ingenious mechanisms that allowed the craftsmen to lay rings of bricks that acted as a horizontal arch – resisting the inward pressure that would make the dome collapse inwards if the resistance were not there. They worked up course by course – and the method worked: the dome is still standing. It could not have buttresses, because it was built up from an existing high wall, and the 'Gothic' profile of the pointed dome means that it pushes outwards less than a shallower dome would have done. Also, in order that the dome would not weigh too heavily, it was constructed as a double shell, connected by ribs – so it is hollow between the inner and outer faces, but they act together to make the whole construction strong and stiff. Brunelleschi could not have found a precedent for that in the Roman ruins.

So Brunelleschi's dome was a triumph of modern ingenuity, in the style of a Gothic cathedral with a pronounced Romanesque character. It was technically brilliant and adventurous – absolutely daring – but stylistically it was not a fresh departure. It was the seamless and harmonious completion of a building that had been designed over a hundred years earlier.

Chapter Five

Renaissance

Born Again

The Renaissance is called the Renaissance because it is supposed to be the rebirth of classical achievements. Vasari started with this version of history back in sixteenth-century Florence, and somehow it has stuck. Of course, as we have seen, there were revivals of interest in the ancient world much earlier than this, especially in Constantinople, and the Holy Roman Empire was definitely a renaissance of some sort.

The particular significance of the renaissance that we call the Renaissance (with a capital R) is that it gives us a label to mark the beginning of the modern era – nowadays historians call it 'Early Modern'. That is to say that it marks the end of the Middle Ages and the beginning of something different. Now, had we been alive at the time the Middle Ages came to an end, we would not have noticed it. We would have thought that things were not very different from how they had been before. But looking back from further away, we feel that we need to designate a break.

In England they say that the Middle Ages came to an end with the Battle of Bosworth in 1485, when the Tudors came to the throne. In France the Hundred Years' War came to an end in 1453, and that is taken as the date of the turn, as it is in the eastern Mediterranean where 1453 is the date of the Fall of Constantinople. In Florence it was 1420 with the construction of the cathedral's dome. There was also in Italy an influx of Greek scholars from Constantinople, familiar with ancient texts.

What underlies this is a slow process of transformation from the feudal order, where hereditary lords raised fighting forces to maintain their domains, which were made productive by a peasant population in a condition of serfdom. Book learning went on mainly in monasteries, and book production meant the copying of texts by hand, which was also done in the monasteries. In the later Middle Ages we start to hear about merchants who made commercial fortunes that rivalled those of the barons, and in Florence there was the extraordinary force of the Medici, who acted as bankers for kings and popes, who were financing wars on borrowed money.

The Medici were important power brokers but often kept themselves out of the public eye so that things were not directly attributable to them. It was Medici money that paid for the cathedral's dome, and they made important commissions from the most prominent artists. They were far from alone in the city with their tastes and cultural aspirations, but they were pre-eminent and not initially part of the established nobility – though later generations of marriages blurred that division.

The architects and artists employed by the Medici and their allies are credited with taking a renewed interest in the ruins of antiquity. Vasari tells us that Brunelleschi (1377–1446) and the sculptor Donatello (1386–1466), who were inseparable companions at the time, went to study in Rome and came back with an ambition to match ancient achievements. This is evident in the cathedral's great dome, though stylistically it owes as much to the local tradition in Florence that might be called Gothic or Romanesque. Donatello's cast bronze statue of David had a huge impact. The date of its creation is not documented, but it is probably from the 1440s, and it was prominently displayed in the courtyard of the Palazzo Medici; it would therefore have been seen by everyone who made use of the building, and was part of the building's rhetoric (Figs 46 and 47). It was the first freestanding male nude statue of the Renaissance,

Fig. 46 Michelozzo di Bartolomeo, Palazzo Medici (1444–60). The principal entrance, leading into the courtyard shown in Fig. 47, is through the arch with a flag flying over it. The arches to each side of it originally had shops in them, but they were blocked up in the sixteenth century when Michelangelo introduced the *finestre inginocchiate* (kneeling windows) with decorative stonework and protective grilles.

Fig. 47 Michelozzo di Bartolomeo, Palazzo Medici courtyard (cortile).

showing the future king, David, as an adolescent – as he is in the Bible at the time he slew Goliath, the giant on whose head this statue is standing.

The new palazzo was commissioned by Cosimo de Medici and work started in 1444. The architect was one of Brunelleschi's assistants, and architecturally it belongs with the secular buildings that Brunelleschi had designed, such as the Foundling Hospital of 1419 (Ospedale degli Innocenti, Fig. 48).

The Foundling Hospital has a famous façade with a run of arches along it making a loggia along one side of a public square (the Piazza della Santissima Annunziata). There is a flight of steps that runs the whole length of the loggia, which makes it quite like a Greek stoa, but instead of an entablature (a straight stone beam) running along the top of the columns, round arches spring from one Corinthian capital to the next.

Fig. 48 Filippo Brunelleschi, Foundling hospital, Florence (1419–45).

There is nothing quite like this in the architecture of the great days of imperial Rome. There, the columns are hardly ever structural, but the arches are. On a triumphal arch, like the arch of Constantine in Rome, the columns are decorative, while the arch springs not from columns but from very solid piers. It is the same at the Colosseum, where the arcades are part of the system of vaults that support the building, but the columns are decorative pilasters. There is a closer parallel in the Early Christian basilica of San Sabina (422–32), where arches spring from the classical columns in the nave. This is unlike the more important basilicas of Saint Peter and Santa Maria Maggiore, where the columns in the nave support a long, flat entablature, as would the columns on the outside of a classical temple.

In fact Brunelleschi's façade for the Foundling Hospital seems to come directly from somewhere much closer to home: the church of San Miniato al Monte in Florence itself (*see* Fig. 41 in the previous chapter). We know it as a Romanesque building, but Brunelleschi and his contemporaries saw it as Roman. It does have reused Roman columns in the interior, and arches spring from their capitals. On its façade there is a row of pilasters and arches that echo the arrangement of the interior, but here they do it in a decorative way – the arches are not structural, but patterns of contrasting marble veneers. Brunelleschi did not need to go to travel to learn from it, and it seems to have informed his sense of proportion and the arrangement of the classical elements. In Brunelleschi's loggia the columns and arches are real and structural, as in the church's interior, and the effect in the façade is very light and graceful.

Brunelleschi

Brunelleschi's major works are two churches in Florence: San Lorenzo and Santa Spirito. They both use repeated square bays with round arches supported either on stone columns or on white walls. They are evenly lit and have a strong sense of geometric order about them – serene places where one steps out from the bustle of the city. The Pazzi Chapel at Santa Croce, also in the city, looks like Brunelleschi's work and has often been ascribed to him.

Vasari tells us that it was Brunelleschi who first worked out the geometric perspective that became so characteristic of Renaissance paintings. He drew some inspiration from Euclid, the ancient Greek geometer, who had written about the geometry of seeing. Pythagoras, with his reverence for numbers and fascination with squared numbers, was another influence. Brunelleschi used Arabic numbers as we usually do today. They had been popularised by Leonardo of Pisa, now better known as Fibonacci (1170–1250), whose name is now associated with a series of additive numbers – but that name was not given to the series until the seventeenth century.

Furthermore there were no decimal fractions for Brunelleschi to use in his calculations: they are another seventeenth-century invention. Fractional quantities could only be expressed as the ratio of two whole numbers – as a half, which is ½, or three-quarters, which is ¾. Some numbers cannot be precisely expressed in that way, and these are called 'irrational' numbers. One example is the length of the diagonal of a square (which is the square root of two, multiplied by the length of the side of the square). Brunelleschi would not have been able to calculate it, but he could draw it and measure the drawing.

Medieval geometers knew that if you take a square and measure its diagonal, then draw a second square with sides the length of that diagonal, then the second square will have twice the area of the first. Medieval masons were fascinated by this relationship, though it seems that Brunelleschi was not. His geometries are rational. The preoccupation with regular geometric ordering and additive composition – building up the whole from a repeated module – seems, in Brunelleschi's case, to derive from ancient Greek treatises, rather than directly drawing on examples from ancient Rome.

The Church of San Lorenzo

The church of San Lorenzo is just across the road from the Medici Palace, and a city block away from the cathedral. The palace's garden door is almost in the Piazza San Lorenzo outside the church, which has an unusual orientation with its main altar at the west. The grand entrance front is also unusual because it is still waiting for the layer of monumental decoration that would give it its expected finish. Instead it is a craggy cliff face of rough-hewn stone.

Fig. 49 Filippo Brunelleschi, San Lorenzo, Florence (1421–42).

The main body of the church is by Brunelleschi, set out on a grid of squares (Fig. 49). At the end near the main altar there are three chapels that contain Medici tombs. One of them – known as the Old Sacristy – is by Brunelleschi. Another – the same volume symmetrically placed on the other side of the church, and known as the New Sacristy – is by Michelangelo (1475–1564), who also designed the library here in the cloisters to the south of the church (the Laurentian Library).

Michelangelo was born near Florence almost a hundred years after Brunelleschi, and established a dazzling reputation there before moving to Rome, where his greatest works are to be found. His understanding of classical architecture was quite different from Brunelleschi's – from a different generation – and we will come back to it.

The Palazzo Medici

The Medici Palace is significant not just for itself, but because other very rich families in Florence saw it as something to aspire to in their own establishments. It was always more than a dwelling for a rich family: it was more like a corporate headquarters in some ways, as visiting ambassadors would come here to do business.

The palace occupies the end of a whole medieval city block. Externally its garden is concealed by a high battlemented wall. The rest of the walls are heavily sculpted with rugged, rusticated masonry that resembles boulders piled up to make something immensely strong (see Fig. 46 in the section above). The upper storeys are progressively more refined and delicate, so they look lighter, but the wall is topped with an emphatic overhanging cornice that reminds us of the building's bulk and gives it a strong silhouette.

The main entrance is through a relatively small doorway set in an imposing arch. There are five of these archways in the façade, and the entrance is not in the central one, but displaced one bay to the left. The other arches look as if they have been blocked up with masonry, and a window set in each. These windows – or at least their surrounds – were a later modification (by Michelangelo) to enrich the appearance of the building – however, it remains quite austere. Originally most of these archways contained shops, which would have made the building's façade seem more open to the street, but they did not open into the palace.

The courtyard is within the zone protected by the outside walls and the guards at the entrance. It is by contrast very delicate, surrounded by Corinthian columns and arches whose co-ordinated span carries the building's upper storeys (see Fig. 47 in the section above). The arrangement is reminiscent of Brunelleschi's Foundling Hospital, but here the arcade has to go round corners. This works by putting a column at the corner, which is rational for the structure, although visually it looks awkward because the arches at the corner run into one another and look pinched. Seen from under the vaults around the edge of the space this is not noticeable, and the columns manage to support the mass of building above, while giving an impression of surprising openness at the courtyard level. This is the courtyard that framed Donatello's David.

The principal rooms are upstairs on the *piano nobile* – the noble level – approached by way of a grand staircase. It is here that Cosimo de Medici conducted his business, in private quarters that were furnished with spectacular artworks, approached by way of ante-rooms where visitors could be kept waiting. Later generations of the family acquired the Pitti Palace on the other side of the river and connected it back to the offices and city hall with a long, covered corridor that helped the Medici to move across the city in a more secure way. The Pitti Palace was much larger than the Medici Palace, but architecturally less interesting. The corridor was devised by Giorgio Vasari (1511–74), who is nowadays best remembered for his biographical writings (the lives of the artists of Renaissance Florence).

He also designed the street with two palace façades facing one another – in these were located the Uffizi, the offices of the city's legislature when it was run by the Medici. It included space that was used to exhibit artworks (including the Medici Venus from the seventeenth century – a genuine antique statue that survived from ancient Rome). Artists who lived in still-medieval cities painted pictures of dream cities laid out on square grids with open space between the buildings, but Vasari's street here was the first such space to be built (1560–81).

The Uffizi was also among the first public art galleries, and was accessible long before they became widespread in the later nineteenth century. The Louvre is the other main contender here, as paintings were made accessible to the public there from about 1681, when the court moved out of the Louvre to the new palace at Versailles. These places are mentioned in guidebooks for visitors – but then so were some private residences where important artworks might be seen by appointment; so it is clear that the boundaries between the private and the public domains were not drawn then in quite the same way as they are today, especially in households with a population of servants living on the premises.

Leon Battista Alberti

If Brunelleschi is seen as the most prominent and daring of the early Renaissance architects, Leon Battista Alberti (1404–71) is seen as the most scholarly. He wrote on a great many topics, including painting. His book on painting was dedicated to Brunelleschi, and it explains the mathematics (geometry) involved in Brunelleschi's perspective.

In my story his most important written work was on architecture: *De Re Aedificatoria* (on building). It was written from 1442 to 1452, and early versions circulated in handwritten copies. Gutenberg's bible was first printed in 1454, inaugurating the era of the printed book in the West, and a printed version of Alberti's book appeared in 1485. The first printed edition of Vitruvius dates from 1486. Alberti's text is modelled on Vitruvius, and like Vitruvius it is

divided into ten 'books', which were always 'sections' rather than independent volumes. Incidentally, when Vitruvius was writing, his books would have been produced as rolled-up scrolls, but Alberti knew the text from hand-written transcriptions on pages as in a modern book (a codex).

There is a story that it was his original intention to produce an edition of Vitruvius, but he soon gave up on the idea. Vitruvius was not admired as a writer, despite the good sense in much of what he has to say. Some of the words he used for technical building terms were not used by anyone else, and no one knew what they meant, so the text had a reputation for being incomprehensible. Also, Vitruvius lived before any of the Roman buildings that one would really want to know about, had been built. All in all it seemed to Alberti that it would be better to start again and try to write something that would be useful to people in his own time, not only architects and builders, but also people who were interested in appreciating and maybe commissioning architecture. It was therefore to be seen as a literary work, not just a builders' manual.

In fact it is the first systematic treatise on architecture to have been written since Vitruvius. Others are known to have been written in ancient Rome, but they have been lost, which perhaps suggests that they were not copied out so often as Vitruvius. During the Middle Ages there were notebooks kept by masons and master builders, but nothing systematic that was designed to be distributed either to the public or within the secretive fraternities that guarded professional secrets. Alberti's book had no illustrations – and neither did Vitruvius's – but some later editions have added them (*see* Fig. 13 in Chapter 2).

At the Palazzo Rucellai (1446–51) we see Alberti's idea of what a noble dwelling should look like (Fig. 50). The building is embedded in a city block, so there is just one façade on the street. An entrance two bays in from the left leads directly to the principal courtyard. The arrangement makes one wonder if there was originally a five-bay façade, with the entrance in the central bay. The stone is treated quite differently

Fig. 50 Leon Battista Alberti, Palazzo Rucellai (1446–51). The first 'modern' use of superimposed orders.

from the Medici Palace. Here the stone blocks are all smooth ashlar, but they are cut with deep joints between each block. There is an emphatic cornice at the top of the building, and two projecting mouldings that run in a clean, horizontal line right the way across, making an entablature for each row of columns – actually pilasters. Structurally this is a solid wall with relatively small window openings in it, but the whole decorative scheme of the façade makes it look as if something more complex is going on.

The arrangement of columns and arches is like that at the Colosseum. The pilasters for each of the three storeys have a different type of capital, and the arches are set within the wall so the top of the arch is well below the entablature, which seems to be supported by the pilasters. This is unlike Brunelleschi's arrangement of them. In front of the palazzo there is a little

piazza, triangular in shape. One side of it is aligned at right angles with Alberti's façade, and there is a small three-bay loggia there, which is configured just as in Brunelleschi's buildings, with the arches springing from the tops of the columns. In an ideal world this piazza might have been squared up, but the practical business of building in a medieval city never overcame the limitations of established, valuable plots of land. The palazzo still feels tucked away, and the diagonal lines of old streets have survived, even though the buildings have been replaced after Alberti's time.

The façade itself remained unfinished – a ragged edge on the right leads one to expect at least one more bay, but presumably the land did not become available while the project seemed important – and then things moved on. There is a real interplay here between an aspiration to build something ideal, and the limitations we come up against in practical life.

The façade here is the first of the Renaissance to use superimposed orders – one row of columns on top of another. The design is meticulous, informed by careful study, maybe of the Colosseum or a theatre building such as the well-preserved amphitheatre at Verona. In Alberti's day the ruins of imperial Rome were mostly not yet excavated, but the Pantheon was in use as a church, and the larger structures could not be missed, even if they were adapted and incorporated into more recent buildings. For example, Alberti did not know the Theatre of Marcellus in Rome, which was properly understood only by later generations. Sebastiano Serlio (1475–1554) wrote about the Theatre of Marcellus in the sixteenth century, and he says that 'just recently' the Massimi, a noble Roman family, wanted to build a house and discovered that they were above the theatre – and with careful excavation and measurement, he could make out its shape. It survives – renovated in the eighteenth century and later – as the Palazzo Orsini, and its walls continue the lines of the superimposed Roman columns down below.

This building shows how our attitudes have changed when it comes to the ruins of ancient Rome. During the Middle Ages they were neglected and left to take their chances. Sometimes the stone in them was salvaged for new building projects, but the city was relatively moribund, so there was no great demand for new buildings. With the return of the popes and the fresh interest shown by individuals such as Alberti, people started to take more notice of the ruins. Now we see them as so precious that we would not touch them with new building work. The aim would be to preserve them as they are for future generations, but in the fifteenth and sixteenth centuries it was possible to take an interest in the relics of the past by incorporating them into a new building, adapting the old building to a new use.

Alberti was scholarly, but had the limitations of the state of knowledge in his time. He thought of the church of San Miniato al Monte as Roman, so his new façade for the church of Santa Maria Novella could make use of the colourful applied marbles that were used there and at the cathedral, and which were indeed from a Roman tradition – but he probably thought of San Miniato as being maybe a thousand years older than it actually was. Also at the base of the façade of the Palazzo Rucellai there are panels of finished stone carved with incised diagonal lines, making a grid of diagonal squares. This is a misunderstanding of imperial Roman *opus reticulatum* – which literally means 'net-like work'. It was used in building big concrete walls. The outer face of the wall would be built using square bricks set on the diagonal, and when they had been built up a little way the core would be filled with concrete. The role of the bricks was to hold the sloppy concrete in place until it set. In principle they could then be removed, but actually they were left in place and covered over with a layer of marble.

By the time the building was in ruins, the marble might have been stripped off to be used elsewhere, and some of the bricks might be visible or have fallen out – and it is in this condition that Alberti would have encountered them. Part of the richness and variety of classical architecture comes from the fact that designers have creatively misunderstood what they were looking at. The aim is sometimes to understand what was done in the past and to try to repeat it, but more often the point is to meet contemporary needs, and if the past can show us how to do that with dignity and nobility, then we can make use of the elements from it that have something to say to us.

Donato Bramante

Brunelleschi and Alberti began their careers in Florence, and visited Rome to study the ruins, and Alberti designed buildings for Mantua and Rimini for important patrons. In Rome the embodiment of the Renaissance was Donato Bramante (1444–1515), who was seen to have brought the ancient Roman architecture back to life. That is what Serlio said about him, and he published drawings of Bramante's buildings alongside drawings of genuine ancient Roman monuments, incorporating him into the canon as a completely authoritative figure.

Serlio's books of architecture were printed from 1537, and historically they are important because they were the first printed books about architecture to be illustrated. They circulated out of Italy into northern Europe, and brought news of the Roman way of doing things to the courts of France and the Netherlands. Bramante's great building project was the rebuilding of Saint Peter's basilica. This involved demolishing Constantine's basilica, which was then over a thousand years old, and a genuine Roman building from the great days of the old empire. The decision to demolish it was controversial, but it was taken.

When the popes returned from Avignon, instead of moving back to the Lateran Palace they established what became known as the Vatican, and Saint Peter's became the head church. Saint John Lateran continued in use, was refurbished, and became ever more splendid in the centuries that followed. Saint Peter's was aggrandised into the headquarters of the global institution that the Church had become. Hagia Sophia at Constantinople was seen as the greatest in Christendom, but in 1453 it had been turned into a mosque, and the Orthodox Church was without its pre-eminent monument. Brunelleschi had shown that great domes were possible in the modern world, and Bramante proposed another for Saint Peter's.

It was a huge project that underwent many changes before its eventual completion, including some fundamental changes to the idea of the design as different architects took charge. Serlio published a plan – which he says is Bramante's – which shows an arrangement based on the idea of a centralised church with a dome, with a semi-dome on each of three sides. The fourth side is extended to make a grand basilica of the space. It is very like the arrangement at Florence Cathedral. Seen from one end the building looks like a centralised domed building – which was one of Bramante's preoccupations. It was what he initially had in mind for the building, and it is what he depicted in a medal that was struck to commemorate the start of the work – a central dome, flanking domes, and a tall tower at each corner of the square over which the dome was set.

The Pantheon is an obvious reference point for the design. As the world headquarters of the Catholic (universal) Church, the symbolism of a centralised space would be apt. But although Bramante and other Renaissance architects often sketched centralised churches, few were ever built because the priesthood always preferred a more directional space for the liturgy – and that is what happened here. By the time Serlio published the plan it had turned into a basilica – but the building was far from complete.

Some Followers of Bramante

Some churches were built with a centralised plan, but they are relatively small. The most famous is the church of Santa Maria della Consolazione at Todi in the province of Perugia, north of Rome (*see* Fig. 51). It is often associated with Bramante because it resembles the kind of project he would have liked to have seen built, but there is no documentation to support any attribution. There is a centralised church at Prato, Santa Maria delle Carceri (started in 1486), designed by Giuliano di Sangallo (1445–1516).

Giuliano di Sangallo also designed a villa for the Medici at Poggio a Caiano (from 1485) in the countryside north of Florence (Fig. 52). It is remarkable for using a temple front on one façade, marking the entrance for the house, which is otherwise at first sight a rectilinear block with minimal decoration beyond a bold cornice and window surrounds. On

Fig. 51 Followers of Bramante, including Antonio di Sangallo the younger, Santa Maria della Consolazione, Todi (1508–1607).

closer inspection it is more complicated than that, but the general idea is a formula that would be repeated many times over during the following centuries. The proportions of the temple front are unexpected, in that the columns seem too short, and they are spaced too far apart. This would not have been a mistake, but can be taken to be referencing the Etruscan temple described by Vitruvius and Alberti, alluding to the early days of Rome.

There were three prominent Sangallo architects: Giuliano and his younger brother Antonio da Sangallo (1453–1534), and a nephew who is known as Antonio da Sangallo the Younger (1484–1546) – despite his name having been Antonio Cordiani. He evidently adopted the Sangallo name to make it clear that he was in the family. They were close to the Medici and the papacy. The older Antonio da Sangallo's household looked after Giulio di Medici as a small illegitimate child. When he reached the age of seven he left to join Lorenzo Medici's household. This Giulio later became Pope Clement VII, and as a young cardinal had a close rapport with his cousin Giovanni di Medici, who was Pope Leo X (there is a painting of them together, by Raphael). The younger Sangallo had the most brilliant career – helped along by his excellent connections – and he would design the papal apartments at the Vatican. Their most famous element, the Scala Regia (the stair that leads up to them) belongs in the next chapter, because stylistically it is Baroque (*see* Fig. 63, Chapter 6).

The older Antonio sometimes worked with his brother, but more often specialised in military installations. He did design a centralised church – San Biagio, near Montepulciano (starting in 1518, after his brother had died). The centralised religious building that Bramante certainly did design – and which is illustrated by Serlio – is the little shrine at San Pietro in Montorio, on the Janiculum hill in Rome, just above Trastevere. It is a tiny building, but intensely wrought, with hardly any space inside it but meticulously designed throughout.

Back to Bramante

The tempietto at San Pietro in Montorio was supposed to be on the site of Saint Peter's martyrdom (Fig. 53). Peter was crucified (upside down), probably at the

Circus of Nero – where Christians were certainly put to death. His burial place was adjacent to this circus, and it was identified (quite plausibly) with the spot where the high altar of Saint Peter's Basilica now stands – but current thinking about the size and orientation of the circus means that no one would now identify the place of martyrdom with the location of the tempietto. Bramante was commissioned to build in the place where medieval tradition put Peter's cross: half way between the pyramid (now demolished) that used to be known as the Pyramid of Romulus, and the one known as the Pyramid of Remus, which is still standing but is known to us as the Pyramid of Cestius – there is an inscription on it with Cestius' name.

Bramante designed an exquisite building that made use of elements of Roman architecture in a completely convincing way. The form of the building derives from the circular Roman mausolea and the martyria of the early church. There is a ring of unfluted Tuscan columns, with a Doric frieze running round above them (which is not shown by Serlio). This is unusual in Roman architecture, but it is organised so there is a triglyph aligned with each of the sixteen columns, and then two more in between. This means that there are three metope panels between columns. They include sculpted symbols of Saint Peter, such as the crossed keys with which he is usually represented (he is supposed to hold the keys of heaven) and the papal tiara (Saint Peter is considered to be the first pope). Each column in the peristyle (row of columns round the building) corresponds with a pilaster on the surface of the cella – the wall of the enclosed part of the building. And each metope corresponds with a coffer in the ceiling of the peristyle – there are two rings of tapered square coffers, with carved rosettes in them, going right round the building.

Niches in the wall of the cella alternate with windows, and in one place the door. Everything is worked out with precision, and adjusted so it all lines up in a radial way round the centre of the building. In the middle of the floor there is a circular hole with a grille over it, so one can see down to the floor below, where there is an ornately decorated crypt – and a hole in that floor that marks the spot where Saint Peter's cross might have stood. Up above, at ground level, the peristyle columns sit on a circular plinth

that is the base for the whole building; beyond this plinth there are three further steps that encircle the building as concentric rings, as they would in a Greek temple. The building sits in the centre of a courtyard associated with the church, and according to Serlio the intention was to set it in a circular cloister – but that was never constructed (Fig. 54).

The younger Antonio da Sangallo was apprenticed with Bramante, and after Bramante's death in 1515 he developed a design for the completion of Saint Peter's. A large model of it survives – large enough to walk around inside it, if it is mounted at table-top height. Sangallo's design used the piers and arches of Bramante's design that had already been put up as the core of the building, but he proposed more layers between that core and the outside. Each of the three apses in Bramante's design had an aisle round it – an

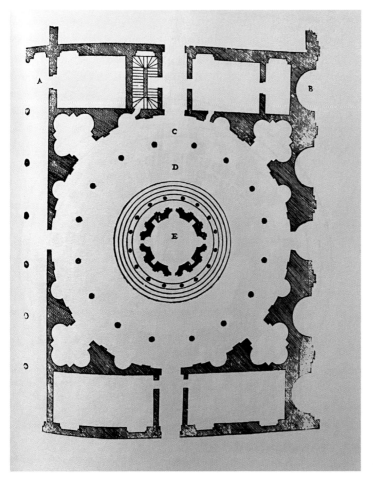

Fig. 54 Bramante's plan, showing his intention to set the Tempietto in a circular courtyard, according to Sebastiano Serlio (published 1540).

ambulatory – and in Sangallo's design the lines of the walls there were carried up through the whole height of the building, as a screen wall with nothing behind it at the top, but with some open arches, so the building seemed to be surrounded by open (but probably inaccessible) loggias. Above this the dome rose as a multi-storey affair, with two arcades encircling it in its lower reaches and then a lantern with a colonnade supporting a steeply conical roof.

The corners of the building were picked out with pinnacles, which were also arranged round the layers of the dome – dozens of them – one for each arch in the arcades, and one for each column in the colonnade. Sangallo had been learning lessons from Gothic buildings. The towers on the entrance front, which would have loomed over Saint Peter's Square and would have been visible from across the city, as the dome is today, look particularly Gothic.

The younger Sangallo died unexpectedly in 1546 (at the age of sixty-two), and Michelangelo was asked to comment on the designs. He had plenty to say, and had strongly negative feelings about the 'German' – which is to say 'Gothic' – character of the work. He offered his services to redesign and supervise the building work without pay, and took over at the age of seventy-one.

The general effect of his changes was to simplify the design, making fewer but larger elements. For example in the dome, instead of two arcades round the base with columns between the arches, in Michelangelo's design there is just one ring of columns, with square-headed windows in between them, and the columns are grouped in pairs, so the rhythm around the dome is less repetitive (sixteen bays take us round the dome, compared with thirty-two repetitions in Sangallo's design). Similarly the columns in the lantern are paired so there are sixteen pairs of columns rather than thirty-two evenly spaced ones, and the visual effect is more stable. Also the curve of the dome is now fully displayed, rather than being half lost behind the arcades of Sangallo's design (Fig. 56).

Michelangelo removed the ambulatories that had been part of Bramante's design, and reduced the overall bulk of the building. Where Sangallo divided up the façades into layers that looked like three monumental storeys using different classical orders – Doric at the

Fig. 55 Michelangelo Buonarotti, staircase in the vestibule of the Laurentian Library – the library of the abbey of San Lorenzo (1523–71). The construction was interrupted, and the work completed long after Michelangelo had left Florence, based on his design drawings.

bottom, Ionic at the top – Michelangelo replaced them with Corinthian pilasters that ran from the ground-floor plinth right up to the building's main cornice (a giant order). The great gains from these modifications are in the much clearer sense of order and resolution in the forms.

Michelangelo certainly knew what he was doing – but something was also lost. Banishing the subsidiary spaces meant that the principal spaces were better lit, and the subsidiary spaces were no longer there for villains to lurk in, as Michelangelo said they would – but at the same time these smaller spaces would have been much more relatable to the human scale. One could have felt well housed in such a space, and could have looked out from it into the vast space of the nave and felt how vast it was.

Something of that effect is achieved at Hagia Sophia, where there are lower spaces at the sides of the huge space covered by the dome, or in some of the great Gothic cathedrals, where subdued lighting and spatial complexity with different scales of spaces give a real sense of the numinous that is in the end lacking at Saint Peter's. The building is so huge it is viscerally unrelatable, and as an architectural experience it is disappointing compared with, for example, Hagia Sophia. One does not appreciate the vastness as an aesthetic thrill. Visually it seems to make sense and is manageable. It is only by walking around inside that one begins to appreciate the sheer size of the undertaking.

The corollary to this – which is good – is that a huge number of people can be in the basilica and feel that they are all participating at the same event because they are all in the same space – a feeling that came to be extended much further with the use that was made of the piazza added by Bernini, and ultimately with broadcast media.

Michelangelo Buonarotti (1475–1564)

Michelangelo's primary reputation was as a sculptor and painter. His idea of what a church should be

was formed by Brunelleschi – by the cathedral at Florence and for Michelangelo more importantly by the church of San Lorenzo, which is more thoroughly Brunelleschi's work, and it has less of the medieval Romanesque about it. Michelangelo knew its regular square bays and its even lighting from an early age. He was thoroughly embedded in the artistic community of Florence, and by the time he was fourteen he was being paid to work as an artist – accomplished enough to graduate beyond the status of an apprentice that would be the expectation for someone of that age. His sensibility was formed in the taste world that the Renaissance had established, so his starting point is rather different from that of the artists a generation or two older than him, such as Brunelleschi.

Michelangelo's first architectural commission was a chapel at San Lorenzo for Medici funeral monuments – now known as the New Sacristy. It dates from 1519, when Michelangelo was forty-four, and work continued until the Medici had to leave Florence in 1527, with only two of the four intended tombs completed. Michelangelo sculpted the tombs, which support figures also sculpted by him – and indeed he adjusted the whole room to make a frame for them. Two figures of members of the Medici clan sit in niches above their tombs, so they are in the room rather than in the tomb. Volumetrically the New Sacristy matches and balances Brunelleschi's Old Sacristy on the other side of the church, but they feel quite different from one another, while being in many ways in accord.

In both sacristies there is a dome, and a need to resolve the curved forms generated by the round Roman-style arches and dome with the square plan followed by the walls. Both sacristies use pendentives to fill the gaps between the dome and the arches below, and they both introduce a circular panel in each curved triangular surface. Brunelleschi makes quite a play of these circular panels. They are used again on the four vertical wall surfaces below the dome, so there is a ring of eight circular panels, four of them vertical, four sloping on the pendentives.

The dome above them is divided by twelve radiating ribs, and the part of the dome between two of these ribs arches up a little, so as to make space for a roundel on the wall as the base of the dome. There are also twelve round-arched openings in the wall above the room's cornice level, and some further round-headed arches as decorative mouldings on the walls below. There seem to be a great many circles and semi-circles in the space, which is centralised under the dome, but opens on one side into a small chapel with a smaller dome of its own.

The preoccupation with geometry is obvious, and again it does not come from the study of monuments in Rome, but from texts about geometry related to Brunelleschi's geometric perspective, and in the pendentives and roundels from Byzantine precedents that could be found in Florence's Baptistery and in Venice at San Marco. However, there is also inventiveness and refinement – taking the historical precedent of the pendentive and making it a very pure geometric figure, so there is a play between the planar and the spherical curved surfaces.

There is little of this in Michelangelo's sacristy. It uses the same materials – especially the characteristic *pietra serena* – a grey sandstone quarried near Florence that can be finely carved – which is used for the main architectural lines in both sacristies. In Michelangelo's the dome is coffered like the Pantheon's, and the walls have arches only above the level of the lower cornice. They are picked out and given emphasis with the *pietra serena*. Below it there are niches in the walls, and some openings – doorways at the corner that allow access – all square-headed forms, most topped by pediments, which are triangular on the windows above the cornice-line and curved (segmental) at the level just below it. The highest windows, just below the level of the dome, have straight tops, but they taper inwards, giving an impression of accelerated perspective, making the space look perhaps a little higher than it is.

The walls are richly modelled. The main architectural lines are picked out in the grey stone – there are pilasters with Corinthian capitals that seem to stand on the floor and run through to support the main cornice, then smaller pilasters above them supporting a smaller cornice. The rest of the walls are covered in carved marble that matches the tombs and their statuary. The wall behind each of the two completed tombs has three tall rectangular niches set in it, the central one containing the statue of the deceased. It is flanked by a pair of pilasters and then by a niche on each side. These flanking niches are quite plain in themselves, but they have a curved pediment and scrolled supports above them as a frame, and then a festoon of flowers carved above that, as though hanging on the wall.

There is a similar arrangement in the corners of the room, where a niche is placed above the doorways. These go up higher than the other niches, and there is a festoon set within each one. The flat wall at the back of these niches is recessed back further around these festoons, as though they were buried in the wall there and the wall has been carved back to reveal them. The effect is very rich, as if ornament has been piled on the wall, but in a very controlled and disciplined way, so it does not seem excessive, but rather as if the whole room has been sculpted.

There is some similar thinking elsewhere in the church, where Michelangelo designed the library – a long, low, corridor-like space – and more sensationally the vestibule with a staircase that leads up to it (Fig. 55). Michelangelo made the designs for these spaces while he was working on the New Sacristy, but it was not finished until much later – by others who interpreted Michelangelo's intentions. The staircase itself is extraordinary. It tapers as it goes up, with an effect of accelerated perspective, but also its three flights in the lower part converge to a single flight that reaches the top, and the central flight's steps are all curved, so it looks as if a viscous liquid has flowed and solidified to make this form. The stair is idiosyncratic and sculptural, and it takes up most

Fig. 56 Michelangelo's dome for Saint Peter's, Rome, seen from across the city.

of the space in the room, completely occupying the centre of it. The walls make a frame for it. The space is very tall, and one enters it from the low-roofed upper floor of a cloister, so the height makes an impact. It makes one want to rise into the empty space in the upper part of the room, so ascending the stair feels like the correct thing to do here.

The verticality of the space is emphasised by the columns that line the walls – six of them on each of the four walls, arranged in pairs, including at the corners where there is one column on each wall. Instead of them standing in front of the wall as a peristyle, they are let into it, so the front of the column lines up with the face of the wall – and they are fully cylindrical columns, not flat pilasters. In between the pairs

of columns there are niches as in the New Sacristy, with pediments over them, and then higher up in the wall further squarer niches with decoration in them. Spatially this arrangement all works to produce the feeling that something important is going on at the higher level.

There is a moulding that runs round the room just above the height of the door through which one enters the space. It establishes a base level on which the columns seem to rest. Functionally the walls are blank, with no actual openings apart from the entrance below the level of the top of the columns. Higher up there is another row of columns, and there are small clerestory windows up there that give the room its subdued lighting.

Sixteenth-Century Italian Work: Mannerist

The reason for dwelling on Michelangelo's works in some detail is that they had great authority and were admired by others, so they established ways of thinking about architecture that would be developed much further by later generations when their style might be called 'baroque'. The other term that comes into use among architectural historians to describe sixteenth-century Italian work is 'mannerist' – when it seems that the architects are reaching for something more turbulent than the repose and harmony of the classic Renaissance artists of the fifteenth century.

The term is used in different ways by different people. Sometimes it seems to suggest that the work is mannered or deliberately exaggerated for expressive effect. Sometimes it refers simply to the period. So for example the architect Andrea Pietro della Gondola, whom we know as Palladio, who was born thirty-three years after Michelangelo and who lived his whole life in the sixteenth century (1508–80), is often called a Mannerist, but his work is as serene and harmonious as any fifteenth-century architect's. There is nothing mannered about it, but he lived at a time when Mannerist artists were around, so he is bundled in with them.

He designed grand houses for the aristocratic estates on the mainland near Venice (the Veneto). The houses were typically the administrative headquarters for an agriculture-based estate, and would include some fine rooms for the landowners while increasing the bulk of the buildings with ancillary accommodation such as barn space for storing the harvest. The owner of such an estate might have a palace on the Grand Canal in Venice for the winter months, while the villa on the mainland would be occupied by the estate's managers and workers through the year, and visited during the heat of the summer until the harvest was brought in.

Palladio was also responsible for some churches in Venice, which will be discussed with the baroque, and most importantly for his subsequent reputation, he also wrote a treatise on architecture – *The*

Four Books on Architecture (1570). Like Serlio, he presented drawings of authoritative ancient monuments (such as the Pantheon and the Maison Carrée at Nîmes), but he also included specimens of his own designs, noting proportions as well as sizes. It would have its widest influence in the eighteenth century in northern Europe, but the ideas that went into it came from the culture of sixteenth-century Italy.

The Renaissance in Northern Europe

The Renaissance in the north of Europe was fundamentally different from the Italian Renaissance because there was a flourishing and very developed tradition of Gothic architecture that continued into the sixteenth century. That tradition was not always abandoned when designers wanted to incorporate ideas from Italy – the new ideas were integrated with the established ways of doing things.

Gothic architecture developed out of the Romanesque, especially in church architecture. Large churches continued to use the basilica form with aisles lined by rows of columns and sculpted capitals, but the buildings were organised around a new vision – spreading from the church of St Denis near Paris – a very rich church where the French kings were buried. The clearest and most ambitious aim of Gothic work was to have the building dissolve in light. The walls were turned into as much stained glass as possible, and the supports were made as fine as possible. For example, take the cathedral at Bourges, where there is a double-aisled space, a huge area of stained glass, and the building's structure is propped in place with huge diagonal buttresses on the outside of the building. Instead of achieving an impressive effect with masses of masonry, Bourges Cathedral dazzles by seeming to be impossibly light. From the inside the buttressing is invisible and one sees a vast space supported by columns that soar, seeming impossibly fine and tall.

There is no work with this sort of character in Florence or Rome, where the proportions of walls and columns continued to be influenced by a classical sense of what was right. The most Gothic work in Italy is in the north, at Milan Cathedral, and in Venice in the older palaces, including the Doge's Palace with its arcades in the lower storeys. At Strasbourg, meanwhile, masons produced an effect of astonishing lightness by building solid walls and then putting a layer of tracery in front of them – supported by the wall behind, but seeming to float free – so the whole building seemed to be made of layers of impossibly delicate stone. It is understandable that the masons of northern Europe did not want to sacrifice these effects just because there were new ideas coming from Italy. They already had good ideas of their own.

National boundaries were quite different in the sixteenth century from how they are now. The king of France held little territory of his own compared with modern France, but maintained control by brokering deals and military alliances with the dukes of various regions and with foreign powers. Until the thirteenth century the dukes of Normandy had also been kings of England. The dukes of Burgundy held territory that ran from today's Netherlands and northern France to the south coast of France, and various dukes as well as the French king entered into alliances with the Holy Roman Empire – this included Spain and arguably briefly England too, while Philip II of Spain was on the throne. He styled himself 'King of England' after his marriage to Mary Tudor, and after her death disputed Elizabeth's right to the throne. Italy was not a unified country then, but had the kingdom of Sicily in the south, the papal states ruled by the Pope further north, and then republics and dukedoms such as Milan (ruled by the French 1499–1526), Florence and Venice – which had an empire of its own, controlling the sea routes to the east.

François I

One of the key figures in bringing Italian style and taste to the north was François I of France (1494–1547). When François became king in 1515 he

visited Milan – as Duke of Milan. Leonardo da Vinci had painted the Last Supper there, and François' most celebrated act of patronage brought Leonardo to France (which is why so many of his paintings now hang in the Louvre).

The Château of Chambord

The most brilliant building for François that shows how the Renaissance creatively met the Gothic-inspired architecture of the French court was the château at Chambord – a hunting lodge surrounded by forest, near other royal palaces on the Loire (Fig. 57). It was never a permanently habitable building, but was visited by the royal hunting parties, which meant several thousand people would descend on the place bringing furniture with them, and would in effect camp out in the vast spaces in the château. The site was completely flat – unlike the sites of the older châteaux, which were feudal strongholds and fortified.

The château at Chambord is laid out symmetrically, with cylindrical towers at the corners. Its plan in outline looks like a fortification because of the towers, but the walls have large windows in them and were not designed to withstand a serious military attack. There are suites of rooms inside, but the major spaces are huge halls that are grouped four-square around a monumental stone staircase. The stair is a double spiral – two spirals interlocked – so in principle it would be possible to have people constantly streaming up one and down the other without meeting. There are sketches by Leonardo of such a stair, but no documents that decisively link him with this one in particular. It functioned as the main circulation between the main spaces, and went up to the roof, where there is a spectacular promenade among the fanciful pinnacles that give Chambord its characteristic silhouette.

The main façades on every side of the château are relatively plain, with square-headed windows and the walls decorated in low relief, with pilasters that

Fig. 57 Attributed to Domenico da Cortona, Château de Chambord (1519–47).

give the idea of classical columns and architraves. The building's distinct character and its fantastical splendour is all above the cornice line, where the steep conical roofs over the towers mix in with decorated chimneys, dormers and lanterns, to produce an effect that seems like a playful miniature city. Some of the pinnacles were large enough to have rooms inside them, and windows suggest upper storeys – but if they were ever used they could only have been reached by ladder. There is something of the fairytale about them. Some of them were used for meals, but there are no kitchens up here, so they would have been more like picnics – with servants fetching the food from a distance for these small informal meetings, protected from the outside world in this magical eyrie.

The architectural language is properly classical, but it is here pushed to a flight of fancy that seems from a distance to be impossibly delicate. In fact it is made from very solid stones, piled up on one another, making a thoroughly Gothic effect like the châteaux illustrated in the *Très Riches Heures du Duc de Berry* (from the late fifteenth century).

François understood how to gain political advantage through making a grand impression with architecture and artworks. His contact with Italy was strong – not only through Milan. His son, who became Henri II, would marry Catherine de Medici, whose family more or less funded the Renaissance, and made commissions that established their enduring prestige in Florence. They were not just artistically significant, but were reputation building for the people who made the commissions. It was that aspect of the works that made the vast expenditure worthwhile in the eyes of the patrons – but François I was no philistine, as is shown by his desire to spend time in Leonardo's company. He wanted to learn from the great thinker as well as to own his works.

The Château of Fontainebleau

On the political stage François' career had its ups and downs, including in 1525 losing the Battle of Pavia, near Milan. The French forces were defeated by the Holy Roman Emperor, Charles V, who was more or less Spanish but very international in his outlook. He already ruled the southern part of Italy (the Kingdom of the Two Sicilies) as well as Spain, the Netherlands and Austria. He took François prisoner and released him in exchange for the dukedoms of Milan and Burgundy. When François returned to France he started making plans for a new palace at Fontainebleau, presumably to restore his sense of dignity. He brought architects from Italy to help with the design, including Serlio.

Comparing the châteaux of Fontainebleau and Chambord, one sees a move from a pinnacled silhouette to something much simpler (*see* Figs 57 and 58). The interiors of Fontainebleau are more richly decorated than those of Chambord, which is a result of it being a more regularly lived-in palace – though its location in the great forest of Fontainebleau also made it a good place for hunting. The simplification is not the result of a more restricted budget – it is an extravagant design and the profusion of ornament is lavish, but the exterior of the building is less elaborate than Chambord. Still, it does not have the simplicity of a characteristic Italian silhouette.

Fig. 58 Sebastiano Serlio and others, Château de Fontainebleau (1528–47, with later additions).

One of the towers from the former fortified château at Fontainebleau was retained in the palace's main frontage that faces the town across a four-square courtyard that is itself unmedieval. The old tower is the tallest element of the entrance front, and it is off centre. The rest of the façade is symmetrical, with a great horseshoe stair that twists in a sculptural way and is more complex than anything known from ancient Rome. The façade is divided into bays, marked out with classical pilasters, and the general run is expressed as two storeys plus an attic. However, alternating bays are taken up an extra storey, giving emphasis to the centre, the ends, and a bay in between. This gives the appearance of a row of connected towers, so there is a lingering memory of the fortified château worked into the classical façade.

The roofline is not elaborately pinnacled, but it does have steep sloping roofs and tall chimneys in the way that was established practice in France, but not in Italy (where roofs with a shallow slope could disappear behind a parapet, and where chimneys were made as unobtrusive as possible).

So despite the architects being Italian, and being brought here to bring their Renaissance thinking to France, the building is characteristically French in its general disposition even though the detail is completely and authentically Italian. As with Michelangelo at Saint Peter's at about the same time, it seems that the Germanic (Gothic) influence was seen as less authoritative than the Roman (classical) ways of doing things – but here in the north not only was there a stronger aesthetic tradition to escape,

Fig. 59 Sebastiano Serlio, Château d'Ancy-le-Franc (1542–50), exterior.

Fig. 60 Sebastiano Serlio, courtyard of the Château d'Ancy-le-Franc. The detail of the stonework is more decorative than on the exterior of the building, with Corinthian capitals for the pilasters here instead of the more robust Doric that is outside.

but also the practical consequences of dealing with a cooler, wetter climate that made imperative such practical measures as well-drained roofs and properly functioning chimneys.

Sebastiano Serlio

The French building in the purest Italian style was commissioned from Serlio at Ancy-le-Franc (1542–50) by Antoine de Clermont, who married the sister of Diane de Poitiers (the mistress of François I's son, Henry II). This was work that only the highest level of society could afford. It is exquisite: absolutely formal – a perfect square in plan, around a square

courtyard, with square towers at the corners, leaving us in no doubt that the building is a château – Serlio published it as 'The House of the Illustrious Prince in the Style of a Fortress' in his Book VI, *On Habitations*.

He describes it as a fort that can withstand an attack with hand arms. It was originally surrounded by a moat on all sides, and each of the towers has small windows in the flanking walls – with a proper classical architrave and miniature pediment over each – which could be used by snipers to protect the building's entrances. It was not left plain as a normal château-fort would have been, but at the behest of the patron was enriched with classical ornament – sturdy Tuscan pilasters on the outside and Corinthian pilasters round the internal courtyard, in an arrangement based on work by Bramante, which Serlio had illustrated as authoritative.

He also illustrated the palace Poggio Reale in Naples, which served as a model for some aspects of Ancy-le-Franc. It, too, is a square building, with square towers at the corners, covered from bottom to top in ornamental classical pilasters – but it has a royal hall rather than a courtyard in the centre. It is not a Roman building, but dates from the time of King Alfonso, when Serlio says Italy was happier and more united (1487). This and Bramante's work are included in Serlio's book on antiquities – but they are not ancient buildings. Meanwhile he mentions that he will not be illustrating the genuinely ancient but barbarous triumphal arch at Verona, because it does not conform with the proper use of proportions.

So Serlio makes it clear that there are proprieties to be observed in the use of classical ornament and its proportion. The point is not to leaf through the books in search of inspiration, but to learn how to do the correct thing so far as form is concerned. He assures us that if we follow his examples the results will be excellent, and he particularly commends his cultivated and powerful client, Antoine de Clermont, for following his advice – and indeed for having the discernment to employ him in the first place.

Ancy-le-Franc is exceptional in France in having an Italian architect working for one of the most powerful men in the country, but it shows a concern to respect the authority of classical style, where most often what we find is a more hybrid take-up of classical inspiration within a tradition that had a very different sensibility. Serlio's work is scrupulous but pedantic. It works as an expression of authority and discipline, but it has none of the fantastical dreaminess of the livelier hybrid work at Chambord, nor the palace at Fontainebleau where he was working with others, and where the vitality comes from a greater enrichment in the ornament and the aberrant inclusion of an old tower and the wayward curves of the entrance stair, which hint at things to come with the baroque.

Chapter Six

Baroque and Rococo

Baroque

The names used for architectural styles are usually given long after the fact. Nobody in the Middle Ages thought they were living in the Middle Ages, and they did not call their architecture Gothic. The same goes for baroque. It used to be a term in formal logic. An over-complex formula (syllogism) that could be simplified into something more direct was called 'baroco', and when the sixteenth-century essayist Montaigne used the term, that is what he meant. He visited Rome and went to mass at Saint Peter's, which was still then incomplete. Today we might call Saint Peter's baroque, but Montaigne did not.

What do we mean by baroque? The clearest way to explain is to take an example: the Co-Cathedral of Saint John the Baptist in Valetta on the island of Malta. It was the seat of the order of the Knights of Saint John, which governed the island and had a military role as well as the expected monastic one. The spaces are set up and decorated with classical pilasters, which are all properly proportioned, and that would have been sanctioned by Bramante or Serlio. But they are overlaid with gilded decorations that enrich every surface with a profusion of ornament (*see* Figs 61 and 62).

Classical architecture is here enriched so much that it seems to have been overtaken by an altogether different sensibility. The pilasters are decorated not only at the capital, but all the way up the shaft. The twisted columns are overgrown with gilded vegetation. The panels in between are encrusted with decorative plants and animals and things that are altogether more abstract, that leave no surface flat, except when the surface is painted, and then the painters try to make us forget the flatness. The cathedral's vaults are painted illusionistically with people tumbling about in the sky overhead, and each altar has a painting over it that suggests spatial depth beyond the surface. One chapel has two Caravaggios in it, including one showing the beheading of Saint John the Baptist, which uses the whole wall of the chapel as a frame for it. It is a sensationally well-endowed building, and the ornamentation is a display of the order's power and wealth that is evident to all.

Going back to Serlio now, the château at Ancy-le-Franc looks severe and pedantic (*see* Figs 59 and 60,

Fig. 61 The Co-Cathedral of Saint John the Baptist, Valetta, Malta. The building was designed by Girolamo Cassar (1572–77), but decorated by Mattia Preti in the later part of the seventeenth century.

end of the previous chapter). Every detail is correct and backed up by precedent, and by comparison (from Serlio's point of view) the décor at Saint John's is overdone and indefensible. It is not something that Serlio would ever have let himself do, even in his most relaxed moments. He would not have wanted to do it. It seems appropriate to say that it is entirely different. However, there is a gradual transition that can be traced over a hundred years that brings us from the sensibility of architects such as Serlio (and Bramante, and Brunelleschi) with their concern to get things right, and the architects of the baroque who were concerned to make an impact in a more theatrical way.

The germ of the idea of the baroque is already in place in the architecture of Michelangelo, where the conventional elements of classical architecture are used in ways that seem to make one feel intense or exalted, rather than serene and rational as in Brunelleschi's evenly lit spaces. The staircase at the Laurentian library is never classified as baroque, because of when it was done, but there are the stirrings of the baroque in it (*see* Fig. 55, previous chapter). Michelangelo's impulses in architecture were expressive, and he enriched the underlying classical order. The impulse of Brunelleschi was to reveal order – to articulate the elements of the building very clearly. The appearance is relatively austere and pared back, the mood calm and rational, whereas the baroque mood is more evidently emotional – enraptured and dramatic – and the detail is piled up in opulent display. It is a style that favours the grand gesture, and suggests that the baroque churches and palaces have the power and confidence to swagger.

The Scala Regia

Another staircase is of interest here: the Scala Regia, which leads up from the piazza of Saint Peter to the Pope's apartments (*see* Fig. 63). It was designed by Antonio Sangallo the Younger, the architect who was replaced by Michelangelo at Saint Peter's. Sangallo died in 1548, so his design was made before then. It

is the stair used when heads of state come to visit the Pope, and it was designed to impress. In the 1660s it was restored and improved by Gian Lorenzo Bernini (1598–1680), who also laid out the piazza with its great curving colonnades (Fig. 64).

The Scala Regia now has an unequivocally baroque appearance. It has columns beside the stairs and a barrel vault over them, and it tapers as it goes up, so there is an accelerated effect of perspective – it looks rather longer than it actually is (and people at the top look rather taller than they did at the bottom). That effect is not unique, but it is better known from stage scenery. For example at Palladio's Teatro Olympico in Vicenza, the stage is set with scenery designed by Vincenzo Scamozzi (1548–1616) depicting streets leading away from the permanent *scenae frons* (as in

Fig. 63 Antonio da Sangallo the Younger, Scala Regia, Vatican, reworked by Gianlorenzo Bernini (1663–66) the stair and its vault taper as they ascend (accelerated perspective). The Pope's coat of arms, flanked by angels, is by Bernini, as is the statue at the foot of the stair. It shows the emperor Constantine. The curtain behind him is sculpted in stone. The panels that look like painting are tapestries by Raphael, which were intended for the Sistine Chapel. The view was drawn by W.L. Leitch, and engraved by E. Challis in 1835. The people are depicted smaller than life-size, which was the convention in views of monuments.

Fig. 64 Gian Lorenzo Bernini, who laid out the Piazza San Pietro with its curving colonnades (1656–67).

a Roman theatre). They could have been flat-painted backdrops using perspective to give an illusion of depth, but they are fully modelled with accelerated perspective so while actors can make entrances through the openings in the *scenae frons*, the streets rapidly become impossibly narrow.

At the Scala Regia the sense of theatre is palpable. Bernini set his statue of Constantine at the foot of the stair. It is a lively statue, showing the emperor in a state of wonder, transported by a vision of the cross. He is on his rearing horse, enveloped in fluidly folded robes, with a huge curtain behind him that is swept sideways by some sort of turbulence, so the whole scene has an air of dynamism about it. The incident was at the Battle of the Milvian Bridge, where Constantine went on to defeat his rival Maxentius, and the vision was a sign that Christ was on Constantine's side – whereas Maxentius had the support only of pagan gods. Its placing here at the foot of the Scala Regia was a lesson to visiting heads of state.

As theatre it works wonderfully well, because the emperor and the rearing horse seem to be responding to the vision of a beam of light from a high window on the other side of the space. There are angels up above the arch of the stair and the Pope's coat of arms, and everything is unified into a set piece. The sculpted curtain does not make much sense within the depicted scene of the Battle of the Milvian Bridge, but it makes very good sense in the room – this vestibule in the Vatican.

Gian Lorenzo Bernini: His Work and Influence

Bernini was also responsible for the baldacchino that covers the main altar at Saint Peter's, placed directly under the dome, which is centred on the burial place of Saint Peter (*see* Fig. 28, Chapter 3). Normally a baldacchino is an honorific umbrella that is carried in procession, perhaps with a person at each corner holding a pole to support the fabric. Here it has been turned into something monumental, cast in bronze, imitating a fabric in the border round the upper part. The corners are supported by twisted columns, based on the Solomonic columns given to Saint Peter's by

Constantine – which are still in this space, surrounding the baldacchino at a higher level under the dome – but Bernini's columns are larger and in bronze and part of an assembly that frames and gives symbolic shelter to the focus of the worship.

He also designed and set out the great curved colonnades that frame the Piazza San Pietro, clearing a great open space in front of the basilica that by then had its Corinthian façade in place – designed by Bruno Maderno, after Michelangelo's death (also visible in Fig. 64, *see* above). The colonnades round the piazza are Tuscan, and open on both sides all the way along, so they do not make a barrier, but a frame, holding back the huddle of medieval buildings and the irregularly disposed mass of the Vatican palace, to make a clearing of classical openness and order within. It was designed as a place for great assemblies, where the gathered crowd could see the pope who could make his address either from the middle of the façade of the basilica, or from a balcony in the papal apartments, which also look out over the piazza. The piazza is now approached by a straight avenue that was introduced in the twentieth century, but in its original formulation it was an enclosed clearing, with the colonnade running right the way round it.

Bernini cut a princely figure as the most celebrated sculptor of the age. In the 1660s he was invited by Louis XIV of France to design the east front of the Louvre, which he did four times over, with daring façades that used classical columns supporting an entablature that curved in plan. It would have made for a striking departure in French architecture had it been built, but while he was in Paris he made such disparaging comments about the state of French architecture and the abilities of the people who designed it that he alienated the French architectural establishment. When Bernini left Paris, expecting his design to be built, the French architects managed to form a committee to redesign the scheme on what they said were 'proper principles'. The result was the east front of the Louvre as we see it today – a straight façade with paired columns running across it, completing a square courtyard behind it – and with a low roof, that disappears from view behind the parapet (*see* Fig. 65).

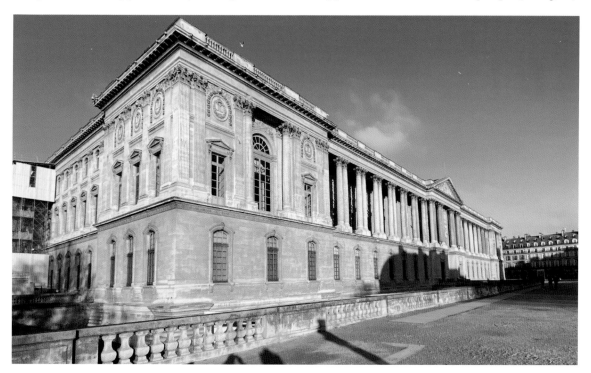

Fig. 65 Louis le Vau, Charles le Brun, Claude Perrault (Le Petit Conseil) and the Louvre colonnade – the Louvre's east façade (1667–74).

Meanwhile Louis' attention had turned to Versailles, leaving the Louvre to take care of itself.

Francesco Castelli Borromini

Francesco Castelli, known as Borromini (1599–1667), was active as an architect in Rome at the same time as Bernini. Where Bernini was flamboyant and arrogant, Borromini was tetchy and depressive. He walked away from projects when he felt slighted, and in the end killed himself. His projects were the most intensely crafted of the era. He had trained as a mason and was adept in geometry, and knew far more about construction and engineering than did Bernini, so his buildings could, and did, make use of spatial intricacy and complexity that was by far the most sophisticated around. He had worked as an architect with Maderno at Saint Peter's, so he was already well versed in the culture of form making in the most impressive of settings.

His first independent commission was from Spanish Trinitarian monks in Rome – a base for them in the capital, and a church dedicated to San Carlo di Borromeo, which has become known as San Carlo alle Quattro Fontane (*see* Fig. 66). It is sited at a crossroad, where two long straight streets intersect. At each of the four corners of this junction there is a fountain, one of them in the corner of the outside wall of the church. These fountains make the crossroads into a little piazza, where one might have lingered in the days before automobiles and the traffic lights that are in place there now. There is a tower above the fountain, but it is almost lost behind a curving screen of façade. The whole street façade of the church's entrance sinuously undulates, alternating concave and convex lines in its entablatures. The four columns are placed in a straight line, but the façade curves between them so one hardly notices.

Inside, the church is surprisingly high compared with its width, and looking up one sees an oval cornice running round beneath a coffered dome, with

Fig. 66 Francesco Borromini, the façade of San Carlo alla Quattro Fontane, Rome (1638–41). One of the four fountains is incorporated in the wall of the church; the others are on the other corners of the crossroads.

coffers in an intricate pattern of octagons, hexagons and crosses. The geometry involved in setting out this dome is complex and related to the projective geometry of perspective. The stone cutter's grasp of this sort of geometry really developed during the Middle Ages with the setting out of the complex shapes of stone ribs for vaults; by the time Borromini was working it was known as stereotomy. Up above – and it does involve a deliberate effort of tilting the head to see it – there is an oval – not the purer shape of the circle – but lower down, although the geometry of the oval is implicit, it is not evident.

Just as the straight line of the columns on the façade goes unnoticed because of the curves of the entablature, so the form of the body of the church is difficult to grasp. One notices columns and altars, everything is in place, but the way things blend together and the curves that deflect our attention make the definition of the space melt away into something uncertain. The effect is profoundly different from that of, say, Brunelleschi's San Lorenzo, set out on a square grid (see Fig. 49, Chapter 5).

San Carlo presents itself as something not so much to be understood, as felt. The harmonious but unfathomable things going on in the lower storey resolve into the precise order of the dome, with its tapering stacked coffers. Light pours down from a lantern in the dome, centred on an image of the Holy Spirit as a dove, framed by an equilateral triangle, which in this context clearly signals the Holy Trinity – remember this commission is from a mendicant monastic order called Trinitarians; the equilateral triangle is also an important generator in the geometry of the plan.

Symbolism is integrated into the architecture in ways that are sometimes apparent, sometimes doubtless hidden in the development of the design. Borromini did not charge a fee for this commission: it was a reputation-building exercise. A statue of Saint Charles Borromeo stands in a niche above the church's main entrance, looking out at the people in the street. He is sheltered by the wings of angels – sculptures integrated into the architecture – and

Borromini's name change seems to cement his association with this building.

Defining the Baroque

There are many stories to be told about the baroque – it is an immensely flexible category of enriched classicism. At its most artistically accomplished it is an expensive style to build: the levels of complexity can be daunting, and the craftsmanship demanded in its execution challenged the best. It became the preferred style for the immensely powerful – monarchs and those close to them – and the church. Rome was the place where the baroque style first took hold, and there are many good examples in the church architecture of the city (Fig. 67).

Bernini and Borromini were the most prominent practitioners, but were far from being the only ones. There are many architects whose work might on occasion look baroque, but who are not usually given that label because of when they worked. For example the most important monument of the English baroque is Saint Paul's Cathedral in London (Fig. 68). It was designed and built at the end of the seventeenth century (1668–1708) when baroque was the dominant architectural style for the buildings of highest status across Europe. Stylistically it is not so very different from Palladio's San Giorgio Maggiore in Venice (1565–1610), designed a hundred years earlier (Fig. 69).

Palladio tends to be labelled as a Mannerist because his working life overlapped with Michelangelo's, finishing later, so he is grouped with other architects of that generation, such as Giulio Romano (1499–1556), whose work at the Palazzo Tè is definitely Mannerist. He takes the Renaissance language of classical architecture and makes it more articulate and expressive, with the use of strong contrasts between rusticated and very highly finished stonework, and eccentricities such as the dropped triglyphs in one of the courtyards.

Fig. 67 A view of the Piazza Navona, Rome, dominated by the church of Sant'Agnese in Agone by Borromini and others (mid-seventeenth century onwards).

Fig. 68 Sir Christopher Wren, Saint Paul's Cathedral, London (1675–1710) interior.

Fig. 69 Andrea Palladio, San Giorgio Maggiore, Venice (1566) interior.

Fig. 70 Andrea Palladio, San Giorgio Maggiore, Venice (1566) principal façade.

There had been painted mural decoration in buildings before the Palazzo Tè (1524–1534), but Giulio brought a new energy to them. They are not the usual depictions of biblical scenes, such as Leonardo's 'Last Supper', but are much more theatrical and disturbing. One room depicted giants demolishing the architecture of the room, and to accomplish the illusion of that effect the wall surfaces were curved to run smoothly into the flat surface of the ceiling so there was no break in the painted surface. It is all-enveloping.

Such illusionistic painting would become a staple of baroque architecture. For example, it can be seen at the church of the Gesù in Rome (1669–1683), where the ceiling painting by Giovan Battista Gaulli (1639–1709) is framed by sculpted stucco by Antonio Raggi (1624–1686), and there is no clear boundary between what is painted and what is sculpted – and the sculpted stucco is overlaid on the expected architectural modelling (Fig. 71). The painting has a spatial effect: it is part of the architecture. It seems to open up a space above the ceiling – and in fact the ceiling seems to have been dissolved away.

The church's architect was Giacomo Barozzi da Vignola (1507–1573), a close contemporary of Palladio, who, like Palladio, is well known for his books about architecture. In Vignola's case (and he is usually called Vignola, despite this just being the place where he was born, and not really his personal name) his best known book is a manual on how to set out the proportions of the orders of architecture – the various columns and entablatures that architects needed to master if they were to build convincingly in the style of antiquity. It was printed in 1562, and its illustrations were used in later editions, including an English translation of 1669: *The Canon of the Five Orders of Architecture*. The explanation was clear and avoided unnecessary complexities, so the handbook circulated widely for centuries.

All the writers of treatises on architecture tended to leave the reader with the impression that there were rules to be followed, as set out in the book, and Vignola in particular, by highlighting the orders of architecture in his book's title and giving their number as five, makes it seem as if there were five ways to be correct about the details of columns. This downplays the variety that is to be found in the ancient world, and in baroque architecture. There is plenty of scope for inventiveness and ingenuity in developing

Fig. 71 Giacomo Barozzi da Vignola and Giacomo della Porta, Church of the Gesù, Rome (1571–75). The mother church of the Jesuits and the epicentre of the Counter Reformation. The architecturally important paintings were added later by Giovanni Battista Gaulli (1679–85).

variations on the canonic patterns, but it is best done later in one's career, after one has mastered the art of getting things correct by the book, by when it might be supposed one's taste is properly formed and good judgements might be made.

Vignola certainly did not anticipate what would become of his church after his death when Raggi and Galli got to work on it. Vignola's façade here is sometimes presented as the first baroque church façade, but it is tame compared with work that came later, and the church registers as definitively baroque mainly because of the work that was added later in the interior. Vignola's instincts as a designer are more sober and canonical, without the restless inventiveness that makes the baroque push past the usual boundaries.

The Counter Reformation

The Gesù is formally the Church of the Holy Name of Jesus at 'the Argentina'. Argentina was the Roman name for Strasbourg, long before it was the name of a country, and there was a tower near here, known as the Argentina or Strasbourg Tower, which was demolished in the twentieth century for the excavation of some Roman temples that are visible there today. The church is the headquarters of the Society of Jesus – the Jesuits – who were very influential in the church's thinking.

Doctrinally the church had been through some upheavals in its time. There were versions of Christianity that were declared heretical and suppressed. That is what happened to Arianism in the fourth century, and Albigensianism in the thirteenth. In the eleventh century the church based in Rome had split with the church based in Constantinople, so from that point we have the Orthodox Church in the East and the Roman Catholic Church in the West – though the name 'catholic' means 'universal', and its aspirations were never limited by any boundaries. From the sixteenth century there was a movement, Protestantism, which did not recognise

the final authority of the Church in Rome. It had a major influence in northern Europe, and for example in England it was adopted as the official state position.

The adoption of Protestantism is called the Reformation, and in England it saw the dissolution of the monasteries, while medieval church buildings continued in use but by a clergy that no longer answered to Rome. The Jesuits are particularly associated with the Counter Reformation – the project to resist Protestantism – and architecture was one of the weapons in that resistance. Under the influence of the Gesù, church buildings were often spatially simplified compared with medieval buildings, sometimes from the outside seeming to be scarcely more elaborate than a barn with some decoration around the front door, with no porch and no transepts – but inside there could be a riot of ornament swept up in the most spectacular theatrical display.

This particular trajectory of the baroque was developed much further in church design, but to understand the appeal of the spaces we need to take note of the fact that the baroque was also developing as the style for the grandest kinds of palace. Vignola was not exclusively an architect of churches, but had also designed the Villa Farnese at Caprarola, which makes the point that individual architects could be involved with both types of building. The style at Caprarola was not baroque, but something rather plainer. The villa was grandiose in conception, but based on a military foundation, and like Ancy-le-Franc, it had projecting towers at the corners that snipers could use to defend the entrances. Unlike most other grand country houses it has a pentagonal plan, based on a fortification. Its internal courtyard is a circle with a colonnade around it, so all directions seem equal – no principal axis is apparent from within.

The Palace of Versailles

The greatest of all the baroque palaces was Versailles, built by Louis XIV and his heirs in the seventeenth and eighteenth centuries. It was far more than a place for the king to live: Louis XIV moved his whole court here from Paris in 1682, and ran France from the palace, with representatives from the aristocracy of every region of France in attendance, acting out their subservience to the king on a regular basis. Back in Paris the aristocratic families had their own palaces – their *hôtels particuliers* – but at Versailles only those closest to the king had anything like that, and the rest had to make do with cramped accommodation within the grand walls. Notoriously there was no plumbing for sanitation at Versailles, and by modern standards the conditions were squalid, but the architectural vistas were grandiose and unparalleled in their opulence.

There was plumbing for fountains – including not only the monumental set pieces such as the fountain of Apollo (Louis XIV was known as the Sun King, and is symbolically represented in statues and paintings of Apollo), but also in intricate works such as the fountain chandeliers in a now demolished Grotto of Thétis (a water-nymph, best remembered as the mother of Achilles). The water jets here looked like candles, and make it clear that there was plenty of know-how about how to control water, but no inclination to use it for services that we would see as more basic.

The most celebrated individual room in the palace is the Galérie des Glaces – the Hall of Mirrors – which was built in 1678–1684 to designs by Jules-Hardouin Mansart (architect) and Charles le Brun (decorative artist, *see* Fig. 72). It extends to a great length, with seventeen tall windows looking out along the principal axis of the palace that extends out for miles into the landscape. The classical architecture here is enriched with lavish ornament and hung with chandeliers, which are reflected in the mirror that matches the windows with external views. They are blind windows, facing a solid wall with the king's

Fig. 72 Jules-Hardouin Mansart, Galérie des Glaces, Versailles (1678–84).

apartment on the other side of it – his audience rooms and more private accommodation.

Part of the point of the room was to make an impression on visitors – that this was a place where unrivalled power held sway. To that end the furnishings, including the chairs, were originally made of solid silver. Later they were melted down to help pay for a war, but they help to clarify the fact that the opulence was not just a matter of taste, but a deliberate assertion of power.

The great thing about the palace is the unified vision of the arts here. The landscape is structured with architectural masses of trees and open spaces that rehearse ideas about vistas and alignments: these would later become familiar in Paris and elsewhere in the masses of buildings (Fig. 73). Here they are masses of trees.

The richly ornamented interiors have painted ceilings that show Louis XIV achieving great things: annexing territory, answering to no one. The king ruled by divine and absolute right, and the paintings proclaim that, in case we need reminding. Spatially the ceilings melt away into sky, with clouds piling up, sufficiently substantial to support the figures who can sometimes fly about, sometimes resting cushioned by cumulus. The ceilings, already high, open up to

Fig. 73 Jules-Hardouin Mansart, the church of l'Hôpital des Invalides, Paris (1671–1710). This is a very prominent building in Paris, stopping the vista across the Pont Alexandre III, which aligns with the Élysée Palace.

give a sense of space beyond them, and their shape is made to help with that effect: they are coved, so the vertical surface of the wall curves gradually to the horizontal plane of the central part of the ceiling, and there is no hard line that the eye can focus on to fix a definite height to the room.

The clouds, mirrors and dangling crystals that reflect and refract the light all cohere to make a space where the boundaries are not too clearly defined, and the effect defies immediate comprehension, seeming magnificently rich and complex.

Background to Versailles: Vaux-le-Vicomte

In France the story that culminates in this room begins elsewhere: at Vaux-le-Vicomte, where Nicolas Fouquet, Louis XIV's minister of finance, bought land 21km from Fontainebleau, and built a château there, demolishing three villages in the process and employing the villagers to work on the new estate. He employed Louis le Vau (architect), Charles le Brun (painter) and André le Nôtre (landscape designer) to design the château and its gardens, which were coordinated in a way that became characteristic in palatial French designs, but which was novel here: a great axis stretching out indefinitely into the landscape, articulated by statues, planting, reflecting pools and fountains, with avenues cut through forest, and a great canal – concealed by the slope of the ground until it is revealed as a vast expanse of water at the last moment.

The mansion is richly ornamented with classical detail, and a great dome over the main garden façade (Figs 74 and 75). There are many statues of people

Fig. 74 Louis le Vau, at the Château of Vaux-le-Vicomte (1656–61).

Fig. 75 Many of the smaller rooms at Vaux-le-Vicomte have illusionistic painted ceilings, and there might have been one here, had the proprietor been able to continue his life at the château. This great hall occupies the central space on the garden front.

inhabiting the stonework and painted on the walls and ceilings. The boundaries between the arts are blurred, and they work harmoniously together. The main building is impressively assertive in its setting, which acts as a frame to enhance the importance of the moated block of the château. The sloping ground was reorganised as level terraces, giving the château several extra storeys of height when seen from a distance in the garden. The gardens are arranged like open rooms, and populated with statues that often have an architectural quality, such as the row of sentinels that keep watch over the main approach,

or the statues on plinths in the gardens that define the edges of spaces.

The story goes that the king came to a lavish entertainment here in the summer of 1661, when Louis was twenty-three. He had come to the throne as a child, but his mother, Anne of Austria, acted as Regent until Louis came of age. Fouquet had come to power under Louis' mother and her adviser Cardinal Mazarin, who died in the spring of 1661. The great spectacle was designed to secure Fouquet's position as Mazarin's natural successor, but there were intrigues against him. Louis was prompted to question how his minister could afford such a display, which outshone the king himself. Fouquet was found to have misappropriated funds, and was removed from all his official positions; he was imprisoned in solitary confinement for the rest of his life.

Meanwhile Louis employed Fouquet's design team for Versailles, to conjure up an even more impressive domain from what was, at that time, still a swamp. In retrospect Vaux-le-Vicomte is therefore to be seen as a rehearsal for the main show, which is Versailles – although in some ways it is artistically more satisfying. The principal building at Versailles has so much accommodation in it that its proportions become rather long and flat, despite the impressive height of individual spaces within.

Ingrained Classicism

The architecture here and elsewhere in seventeenth-century Europe was well rehearsed and highly codified. The orders of architecture as described by Serlio, Palladio and Vignola, are taken as read, and are used with the prescribed proportions. They were adapted to the practicalities of domestic architecture, with windows and doors placed so they made sense in a disciplined way, using symmetry and the regular placing of columns as the basis of architectural order. Doors that would be used in formal movement between rooms, maybe in procession, would be aligned ('in enfilade') and their architraves elaborated with carving – mouldings, swags, statuary, over-door paintings. Doorways that were functionally necessary but that would not be used by important visitors. There were also the servants' doors that led into passageways and modest stairs that allowed circulation from the service quarters. They would be made almost invisible, and are worked into the design of the building without having an architectural expression.

In grand houses of the seventeenth and eighteenth centuries the baroque style of decoration would be supplemented by liveried servants – footmen –

standing in matching pairs on either side of the grand portals. They were chosen for their looks and dressed in the household's colours. They were people, of course, but they were treated as though they were part of the architectural décor – part of the continuity of inhabitation that moved from the relaxed and free-floating postures of the painted gods, to the stiffer and more formal statues along the cornices – and then these actually living footmen, who would be generally immobile, would spring into action if a pair of doors needed to open. They were part of the place's system of security, and would make clear the status of the house.

Rococo

One of the outstandingly accomplished places in this general manner is the palace of the Prince-Bishops of Würzburg, now in Germany. Stylistically it is called rococo rather than baroque because there was a change of mood in the décor from the ever-richer baroque to a search for a lighter effect. The aim seems to be to dematerialise the building, and make ambiguous the boundaries between the real and the illusory.

In the great staircase hall at Würzburg there is a painted ceiling by Giambattista Tiepolo, who was brought from Venice to paint it. It is larger than the ceiling of the Sistine Chapel, and as rare an accomplishment. When seen from the staircase the ceiling seems to open up to the sky. We know that it is painted of course, but it is not clear where the painting begins. There is a real cornice running round the top of the stone part of the wall, with a projecting edge that marks the beginning of the paintwork, on a coved surface that curves over from the vertical of the wall to the horizontal of the ceiling without a hard edge between them. The most solid-looking terrestrial figures are grouped in the lower part of this coving, and they seem to sit and stand on the cornice and the parapet above it, which is painted but is nevertheless part of the architecture.

Elsewhere the architecture is projected up into the illusion space of the painting – there is a pedimented gateway that is certainly a part of the architecture of the staircase hall, but it is entirely painted. Moving in the opposite direction there is a painted life-size dog that seems to have wandered on to the cornice and to be standing outside the painting's 'frame', and elsewhere a fully modelled painted limb projects from the surface to complete an otherwise flatly painted figure. The border between building and painting is completely confounded, and the eye cannot make accurate judgements just by looking at the work.

Elsewhere in the palace there is decorative plaster-work that takes on a surprisingly abstract quality. Its lively curves take up asymmetrical shapes, and they tend to be painted in light, sugary colours, or shades close to white. The aim is a lightness of touch, and the style is especially associated with places where gaiety is in demand – ballrooms and places for parties, for example. Nevertheless the outstanding examples of rococo architecture that survive are to be found in church buildings.

The Wieskirche in Bavaria for example, by the Zimmermann brothers, looks as if the whole place has been animated by a whirlwind that has shaken everything out of the shape it had when everything was still (*see* Fig. 76). It is in a small village, Steingaden, which had an agricultural population, but there is a miraculous statue here that performed miracles and attracted a stream of pilgrims, so it had visitors from further away. This kind of church is part of the Counter Reformation project to draw people away from Protestantism.

The outside of the building is simple and does not draw attention, but the inside is spectacular in the most theatrical way. Artistically it is very accomplished and the engineering is very sophisti-cated, though it usually goes unnoticed. We accept

Fig. 76 Brothers Johann Baptist Zimmermann and Dominikus Zimmermann, Wieskirche, Steingaden, Bavaria (1745–54).

the painted surface's story about it having been dematerialised, and forget how much timber is up there in huge trusses that are arranged to counterbalance one another and allow the spaces to flow into one another, and for arches to wander in plan as they leap across the openings they frame. A naive arch-builder trying such a move would find the arch falling forwards, rather than acting as a support. There are miracles everywhere in the way that gravity seems to be held in abeyance.

Just as important as the direct aesthetic value is the fact that this was the style of architecture used in royal palaces and the houses of the highest aristocracy when they were displaying their finery to one another. It is high-status architecture that is used here in a context that made it accessible to the most modest peasant, and its appeal right across the social range – from rich to poor and educated to credulous – is the reason for its usefulness to the Church. The labourers from the farms would never have had access to this sort of vision had it not been for the church, and it was inspiring and uplifting in ways that might not be religious in themselves, but the feelings could be harnessed in the service of spirituality.

Iberia and Latin America

Baroque architecture was ingrained in the culture of Spain and Portugal during the seventeenth century and later, and it was exported to the Spanish and Portuguese colonies in America not only in official buildings but also in churches where missionaries went to spread the gospels to indigenous people and to support the settlers who were already Christian. Missionaries also took baroque architecture to India – for example, in the late seventeenth-century Portuguese church built around the relics of Saint Francis Xavier, an important Jesuit, who died at Goa en route to China.

In the same way that the Roman Empire had spread classical architecture across the territory it controlled – including most of Europe, the north African coast and parts of Asia – the dispersal of baroque into the Iberian colonies and through the Jesuit missions made baroque into the first global architecture. There are examples of baroque buildings from Spanish and Portuguese influence to be found not only in former colonies such as Mexico and Brazil, but also in the parts of Mexico that have subsequently been overtaken by the United States, such as Texas and California.

The consequence of this global spread is that baroque buildings are most likely to be the first buildings from a classical background that are encountered by the greatest number of people worldwide. One way of organising a book about classical architecture would be to take the most familiar version of it and then look at its antecedents and its developments. The book in your hands now is organised broadly chronologically up to this point, but when the architecture is so widely spread it is only to be expected that different narratives develop. For example once we have a clear idea of the baroque, we can go back and revisit ancient Roman architecture and find that there was design in the ancient world that we would not hesitate to classify as baroque had it been built 1,500 years later.

In a way Borromini knew this. His designs used elements that are to be found in ancient Roman architecture. Some elements, like the Corinthian capitals, are normal and canonic. Others, like the curved cornices, are found rarely, but they are there (at Hadrian's villa at Tivoli). Borromini's pointed pinnacle domes have a precedent in far-flung ancient tombs.

The baroque inclination is to elaborate and embellish, to adorn and dissolve, and it is not confined within a defined period. The term is stylistic rather than defining a bounded era that has a definite beginning and end – but despite that, references are made to 'the age of the baroque', and when people do that they mean a period that begins in the sixteenth century and ends in the middle of the eighteenth. However, there are important baroque buildings from later than that, and they can be labelled as neobaroque, but it is the same sort of architecture, just being built at a different time. Also by then there were clear stylistic alternatives – the baroque was not the style by default. During the nineteenth century, for example, the Gothic came to be a very regular choice of style for church buildings, while the baroque was used for theatres – and royal palaces, one might add, though there were not so many of them.

Linderhof

Two finely designed baroque palaces were built for Ludwig II of Bavaria. One, Linderhof, is compact and sits in the foothills of the Alps, more as a retreat than a place for formal receptions (Figs 77 and 78). Its classical design is as enriched as can be, with a

Fig. 77 Georg von Dollmann, Schloss Linderhof Ettal, Bavaria (1874–86).

build-up of ornament around the axis of the entrance façade, and then the interiors are covered in gilded plasterwork and chandeliers, so there is barely a flat wall surface to be seen. The grounds are landscaped with a fountain on axis with the main block, and then walks take one out into the pleasure grounds that include relatively small pavilions in different styles – a Moorish kiosk, a huntsman's hut arranged around a living tree with spreading branches, and a cave with pioneering electric lighting.

The building work here is less extensive than that of the Petit Trianon at Versailles – one of the smaller palaces in the grounds there, which was adopted by Marie-Antoinette – but it owes something of an imaginative debt to it. Where Marie-Antoinette played at being a shepherdess, Ludwig played at being a huntsman, or at least encountering one. These settings were informal, and where the king came to escape his court. The style of the house, though, is of a grand palace in miniature. The bedchamber is much more elaborate than that of the Petit Trianon, and is modelled on the king's bedchamber in the principal palace at Versailles: this was the bedchamber in which the king did not actually sleep – there was a more private room for that, behind the scenes – but where he was officially put to bed and where he conducted his levées in the mornings.

Ludwig's bedchamber was actually private, but looked like a place to conduct elaborate court ritual. He was in fact a king, but in his imagination he was role-playing being an absolute monarch some of the time, and then slumming it with the locals at others – and the architecture was built so his imaginative world was externalised and remains visible to others.

Ludwig's best-known palace was Neuschwanstein – a fantasy medieval fortress on top of a mountain overlooking a ravine with a spectacular waterfall. It has Romanesque and Byzantine elements that one could co-opt into a story about classical architecture, but its imaginative world is thoroughly medieval, refracted through Wagner's operas. His other baroque palace was at Herrenchiemsee, on an island in the lake, and it was a version of Versailles, with a spectacular hall of mirrors that was intended to outdo the original by being slightly longer (Fig. 79 – compare with Fig. 72).

Artistically the achievement involved in making a reproduction is imaginative, not in the vision that

Fig. 79 Georg von Dollmann, the hall of mirrors at Neues Schloss Herrenchiemsee, Herreninsel, Chiemsee, Bavaria (1886).

is to be realised, but in finding the resources and materials to achieve the same effects as before in a different place and with more advanced technologies.

The reason the building matters in my story is that it shows how strong a hold the baroque had on the imagination. It seemed very powerfully to be the right thing to have in order to have a setting that showed one as a king. The role is genuinely theatrical: acting out the part of the king is what a king does, and the architecture helps to provide an appropriate setting. It is this aspect of things that accounts for the enduring use of baroque in the accommodation that people commission when they want to be seen as powerful: for example General Franco in Spain, Nicolae Ceausescu in Romania, Ferdinand Marcos in the Philippines, Saddam Hussein in Iraq and Donald Trump in New York have all, in the twentieth century and after, presented themselves as dwelling in more or less baroque settings.

Baroque and the Theatre

In describing the baroque as a style, I keep wanting to reach for the word 'theatrical', and it was in the theatre that the baroque has been normalised since the nineteenth century. For example the municipal theatre of Sao Paolo in Brazil was built from 1903 to designs by a local architect, Francisco de Paola Ramos de Azevedo (1851–1928) (*see* Fig. 80). He studied in Belgium, but returned to Brazil to practise as an architect.

Contemporaneously an opera house was built in Mumbai to designs by Maurice Bandmann and Jehangir Framji Karaka. Bandmann (1872–1922) was a theatrical impresario, born in the USA, who travelled extensively commissioning theatres and producing entertainments in Simla, Kolkata and Madras. He brought Italian opera to the Indian

Fig. 80 Francisco de Paola Ramos de Azevedo, Municipal Theatre, Sao Paolo, Brazil (begun 1903).

stage, presumably mainly for the colonial expatriate populations. Karaka was a very prosperous local businessman, but documentation about him is lacking. He was Parsi–Zoroastrian, with ancestry in Persia – and Bandmann found that Parsis were enthusiastic theatregoers compared with other social groups in India. Baroque classicism sits comfortably alongside the elaborately decorated traditional Indian architecture, and there seems to be real affinity here – but Bandmann was bringing a Western model of the theatre and the architectural style that went with it.

The apogee of that style of theatre design was Charles Garnier's design for the Opéra in Paris (Fig. 81). There are other theatres where great works have been performed and that have cultural significance, but nowhere in a modern city is there a theatre – essentially an inward-looking building type – that has such a presence as an event in the urban fabric. It was constructed between 1861 and 1872, when Paris itself was being reconstructed with new boulevards under Napoleon III and Baron Haussmann. The opera is the end point of a grand avenue that goes directly

Fig. 81 Charles Garnier, the Opéra, now known as Opéra Garnier, or the Palais Garnier, Paris (1861–72).

to the Louvre – specifically to the wing of the Louvre where Napoleon III's Minister of State was installed with an apartment and reception rooms that exactly match the baroque of the opera – which soon became known as the Palais Garnier. It is indeed like a palace.

In more modest theatres the focus is the stage, and the auditorium is arranged to give as many people as possible a decent view of it. The rest of the building is usually subservient to that, so the performers might be crowded into barely adequate accommodation, and the audience might be herded into position and then have to queue at the end as they disperse. The Palais Garnier makes lavish provision for all the expected activities. The spectacle on the stage is supported by huge machinery that could raise scenery into place, or fly it up into the fly tower using counterweights.

The volume of the auditorium is unexceptional, but it is lost at the heart of the building, with as much space above it, below it and to the sides, for the sake of scenery, and a huge block of accommodation for the actors, stage hands and management. The building is an independent block surrounded by streets, so the back of the building is very apparent, and it is clear how much of the building is inaccessible to the visiting public – though not so clear how much of it there is also underground. It is in this hidden zone that Gaston Leroux imagined the fictional *Phantom of the Opera* (1910).

In addition to all that there is a vast volume of space given over to the audience to wander round in, to consume food and drink, and to put themselves on display as they lingered in this fantasy world that is in between being public and private. The theatre in many a city is a place where people would go to be seen. In Venice, the Fenice Theatre put on a documented spectacle in which the dukes and duchesses of the northern Italian regions dined at a large table on the stage, while an audience watched them. In Paris the opera raised this type of spectacle to an unscripted performance on a regular basis, and gave it an appropriate setting. Architecturally the most lavishly decorated part of the building is not the auditorium, but the main stair between the ground floor and the smartest tier of seating. To walk up or down this stair while the Emperor was in the building would have been as much of a performance as anything that happened on the stage.

The baroque is classical architecture that has been enriched and where the elements tend to merge in a sculptural way, so there is a sense of fluidity in the ensemble, often with sculpted figures animating the décor. At the Palais Garnier these sculptures are particularly good and lively. The taste for the baroque is often evident, and is not always brilliantly executed – perhaps for want of money, or because the right sort of artists were unavailable. When the baroque goes wrong it can look trashy and overburdened, weighed down by opulence that seems misplaced. But when it is done to perfection, as at the Wiesskirche, it seems to be animated by a rushing wind that sets the spirit free to soar through its painted heavens.

Chapter Seven

Neoclassicism

Post-Baroque Classicism

The word 'neoclassical' means 'new classical', and it does not always mean the same sorts of building. Archaeologists who are accustomed to dealing with the ancient world can think of any classical building from the modern world as neoclassical, and – as historians will tell you – the early modern period begins at the Renaissance. Art historians tend to use the term specifically to refer to the taste for austere simplicity associated with the style of Jacques-Louis David's paintings, such as the portrait of Juliette Recamier (1800), which shows the sitter against a bare background, with bare feet and very simply dressed.

In architecture the clearest statement of what neoclassicism was about was made by a priest who worked at the court of Versailles and who was therefore in daily contact with the most enriched baroque architecture. His name was Marc-Antoine Laugier (1713–69) – he was often called the Abbé Laugier – and in 1753 he published his *Essay on Architecture*. Neoclassicism came to be associated with the French Revolution of 1789 and with Napoleon, but its clearest statement comes from a generation before the revolution and from a priest at the court, who would not have been in sympathy with the revolutionaries. He wanted to see reform in architecture, and his project was to remind people of the fundamentals of architecture, which seemed to have been forgotten as the ornament had taken over.

The second edition of the book had a frontispiece that brilliantly established his argument in a single image (Fig. 82). It shows what purports to be the origin of architecture: a primitive hut that resembles the general shape of a Greek temple. Its four columns, one at each corner, are living trees, still growing from the

Fig. 82 Charles Eisen, the frontispiece to the second edition of Marc-Antoine Laugier, *Essai sur l'architecture* (published 1755).

ground. Its roof is made of roughly hewn branches. The building is stripped back to its essentials – and beyond. Laugier said that the beauty of buildings comes from their columns, and they should be fully modelled in the round. He condemned pilasters, and even walls were allowed only because they were useful, not because they could contribute anything to the beauty of a building. Unpretentious buildings with no claim to aesthetic merit could use walls freely, but had better avoid any suggestion of columns rather than do them half-heartedly.

In other words, Laugier was positioning the Greek temple with its peristyle back at the centre of architecture, displacing the Roman elaborations of the temple form – the pseudoperipteral temples with pilasters, the Colosseum's use of the orders as decoration but not as structure. Columns were to be real, and they were to support a real entablature, not be reduced to flat representations of such things on a wall that was the real structure.

Maybe this sounds absurd and impractical, but it could usefully inform the imaginative thinking of architects. Sir John Soane (1753–1837), whose house and office survives substantially intact and stocked with the things he owned, had an impressive library that included several copies of Laugier's essay for the use of his students. The effect of the essay is a call to order – to remember that beneath the decorative scheme there is an idea of a structure. Although Laugier was talking about architecture in general in the essay, it is clear that what he had in mind principally was the architecture of churches, and his model of an architecture of well-modelled columns repeated through the space was something that Brunelleschi would have recognised but the Zimmermann brothers might not.

The way of thinking that is crucial to the neoclassical architect is a desire to be correct – to know the rules and to be seen to follow them, in order to have authority on one's side. This contrasts with the baroque sense of abundance, where the overriding aim is to put on a good show. These tendencies – one ultimately leading to exuberance, the other to pedantry – are not confined to a distinct period of time or place, and might even fluctuate in the mind of an individual architect.

There is a tendency in people who write books about architecture that try to codify things, to try to make sense of the complexity before them by devising some rules that help the reader or the writer to find a way through the material. Palladio, for example, has a tendency to see the art of building to be governed by harmonious proportions with simple ratios (the cube, the double cube, and so on), and his architectural vocabulary tends to use standard components, harmoniously adapted to complex circumstances.

This might make Palladio's designs sound formulaic, and in reality they are saved from that by their varied sites and states of preservation, but there is a book – George Hersey and Richard Freedman, *Possible Palladian Villas* (MIT Press, 1992) – and a computer program that show how straightforward it is to generate thousands of possible designs by feeding in a few parameters. The designs are all plausibly Palladian, and are literally formulaic – produced by algorithms. Similarly if one were to adopt Vignola's canon of the orders, a standard sort of classical architecture would be produced that would be correct in every respect, but lacking in originality or vitality.

One of the things that gave scope for originality within a neoclassical mindset was that archaeological discoveries kept being made, and they extended the architects' repertoire. The most important publication for neoclassicising architects was Stuart and Revett's great multi-volume work *The Antiquities of Athens*, published by the Society of Dilettanti in London on large (folio) pages with compelling and accurate representations of key monuments from Athens, most of which were known by reputation without their precise characteristics being accessible. The first volume came out in 1762.

Post-baroque neoclassicism is informed by Greek models in a way that the architecture of the early Renaissance simply could not have been, because of the state of knowledge at the time. Again the architects of the eighteenth and earlier nineteenth centuries did not call their work neoclassical – the term they tended to use at the time was 'Greek' ('Grec' in French, 'Grecian' in English). In the painter David's work, associated as it was with Napoleon, the Spartans' military culture was recognised as well as the philosophical and literary culture of Athens. One of David's largest and most complex paintings is of the Spartan leader Leonidas at Thermopylae, where he led his band of 300 élite warriors to their heroic deaths for the sake of the state, which was saved by their sacrifice.

The archaeology could inform the depiction of Spartan austerity as well as Athenian luxury, and anything in between. However, before going further into the Greek aspect of the architecture, I will return to the pre-Revolutionary world and Laugier's call to remember the fundamentals of architecture.

Romantic Fundamentalism

Laugier's fundamentalist thinking ties in with a wave of cultural change that was sweeping Europe, and which came to be called Romanticism. It is often tied to the figure of Jean-Jacques Rousseau (1712–1778) from Switzerland, whose first published work was a prize-winning essay recognised by the Dijon academy in 1750: his *Discourse on the Arts and Sciences*, which argued that we would be better off without them (the arts and sciences). He believed that people were naturally good and that civilisation corrupted them away from this natural goodness.

This concern to look for natural goodness in the origin of things became a major theme in the art and culture of the later eighteenth century into the nineteenth, which is sometimes called the Age of Romanticism. It is one of the reasons for the interest in Greek archaeology, because Homer was the earliest known literary text, and Greece was often seen as the origin of civilisation; also the Greek language was seen as the language in which human thinking first developed. It was a view that could not be sustained as new discoveries were made in the wider world, but Greek art and culture were admired by the Romans in the ancient world, and it was known that Greek culture lay at the root of Roman culture.

The Greeks were known to be more closely in touch with nature and to the source of things. Rousseau's speculations, though, reached back much further, and tried to imagine the origins of things as a matter of logical necessity, or at least of psychological plausibility. For example, when he was speculating about the origins of language, he imagined that there was a time when humans communicated without there being defined words. The grunts and sighs that we might share with other animals became systematised first into musical sounds, and Rousseau imagined a transitional phase in which people expressively sang to one another. He went on to have a great if controversial reputation as a political theorist, but before that he was known principally as a composer, whose work was popular and much performed. It was based around folk tunes with expressive melodies and little interest in harmony.

Today Rousseau's music sounds trite, and if it is ever performed it is for its historical, not its musical interest. But music is often present in Rousseau's thinking. By contrast he did not have much to say about architecture – but he had no need because Laugier had already speculated just as Rousseau might have done. For example, Laugier imagined that the vaults of the Gothic cathedrals might have been inspired by avenues of trees – an idea that has no historical justification. The idea did not circulate until the eighteenth century, and however plausible it might seem, we know that historically the building form derives from the Roman basilica, which has no resemblance to an avenue of trees. The proliferation of ribs in fifteenth-century vaults made the resemblance closer, but it seems to have been accidental. It is only with eighteenth-century speculation that the idea is made fully explicit – for example in James Hall's willow cathedral of 1792, or the church of Saint Nikolaus in Leipzig, where the capitals from the 1780s sprout palm fronds that start the vault's ribs on their way.

Marie-Antoinette's personal engagement with these ideas saw her wanting to lead a simpler sort of life than the court allowed, so she developed a private domain around the Petit Trianon accessible only to her friends, not to officials. The Petit Trianon palace was itself a neoclassical building, designed by Ange-Jacques Gabriel for Louis XV and his immensely powerful mistress Madame de Pompadour. It was set up to be a place of escape, and its décor was lighter in mood than the baroque of the state rooms – charming and graceful, rather than deliberately imposing – but still a royal palace that leaves one in no doubt about the status of the occupant.

By contrast, the so-called hamlet that Marie-Antoinette commissioned and which was built in the gardens to designs by Richard Mique (1728–1794) in the 1780s was designed to look rustic in a picturesque way, and the set-up included some farm animals as part of the *mise-en-scène*. Although the hamlet looked like a small rural community, the buildings functioned as a single dwelling, its rooms dispersed into separate buildings – so for example, one building that looks like a cottage functioned as a kitchen, with a double-height space within the building's envelope, and another cottage was a billiards room.

Another was a dairy. The queen liked to dress as a milkmaid, a role-play with erotic connotations that are made explicit in the ceramics made for another dairy, at Rambouillet, where fine porcelain milk bowls were made in the form of a delicately tinted human breast. This dairy is in a classical style, designed to keep milk cool even in the heat of summer, so there are no windows in the walls and all the illumination comes from rooflights. The entrance façade is in rusticated stonework with a rusticated column on each side of the door, which has a segmental pediment over it. It looks sober and sophisticated and more like a small institutional building than a dairy, but in the pediment there is a sculpted roundel showing a suckling calf.

Inside the door there is a spacious porch with a coffered dome over it, with rosettes in the coffers (as there used to be at the Pantheon). The dome is contained within the roof space of the building and does not show from the outside, so it is quite unanticipated. However, the *coup-de-théâtre* comes when one leaves the grand porch and enters the building's main space (Fig. 83). This is dominated by a wall of irregular rocks, which once had water flowing down them, making a grotto with a white marble statue of

a woman with a goat. The water had a cooling effect on the space, which has a coffered barrel vault. The statue represents the goat Amalthea, who suckled the infant Zeus, and was sculpted by Pierre Julien in 1787, with a gratuitous nymph.

Panels on the flanking walls are very finely sculpted in low relief; in one, Apollo is shown guarding his flock of cows (while Hermes makes off with some of them), and in the other the infant Zeus is shown suckling from the goat. The imagery of every part of the dairy is classical through and through, but the rock formation marks an architectural fundamentalism that signals a new start. The dairy is decorated in a way that is lavish in terms of effort and quality, but is visually austere.

A short walk away there is a little house that was decorated for the queen's friend, the Princesse de

Fig. 83 Jean-Jacques Thévenin, Dairy (*Laiterie de la Reine*), Rambouillet (1786).

Fig. 84 Nicolas-Quinibert Foliot, sea shell interior, Rambouillet (1780).

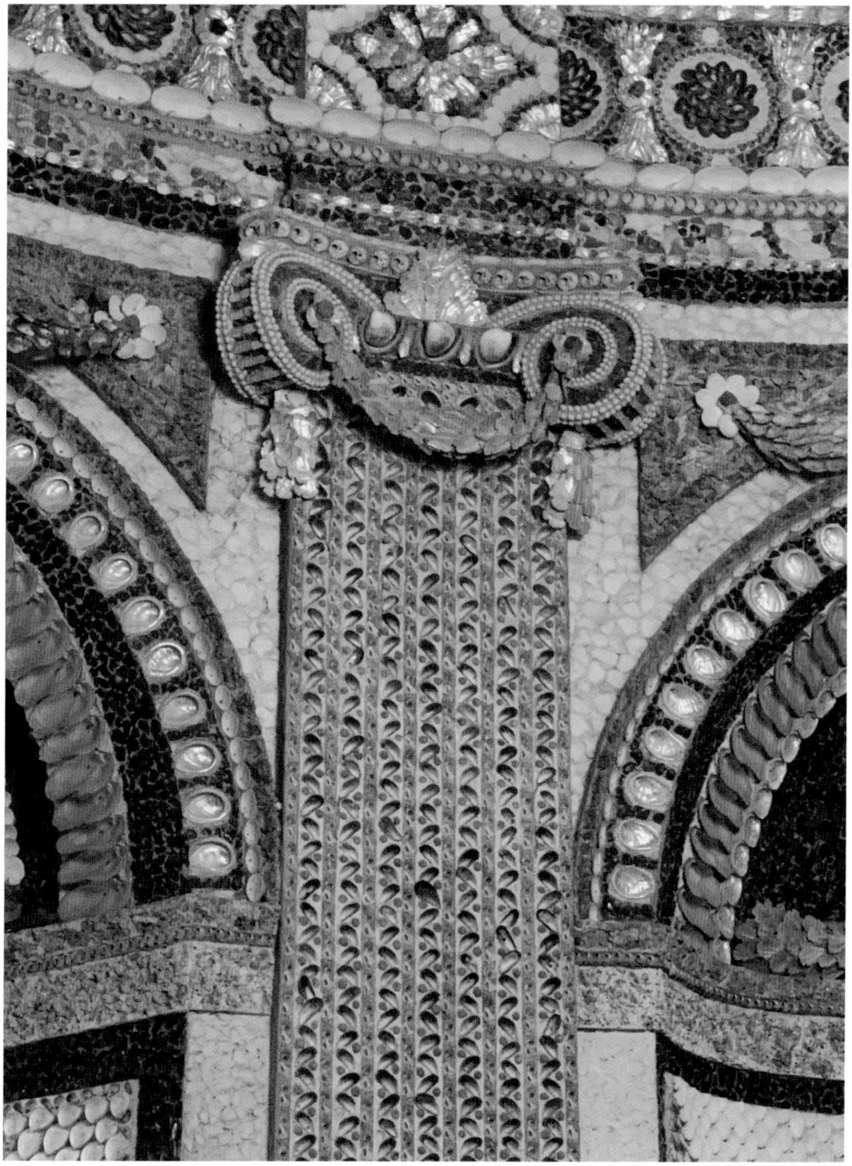

Lamballe; the interior is covered in sea shells, organised to make a version of classical decoration (Fig. 84). Where we would expect to see mirrors, we find iridescent panels made from mother of pearl, and Ionic capitals and pilaster shafts made from mussel shells. Oyster shells hang from the chandelier. It is another exercise in the primitive – a sophisticated person commissioning something that is both modest and extravagant. The materials of the decoration would be thrown away from the kitchens, but their arrangement and design are the work of skilled artisans spending countless hours on the work.

Claude-Nicolas Ledoux

The most monumental expression of this kind of primitivism is in the work of Claude-Nicolas Ledoux (1736–1806) at the Royal Saltworks at Arc-et-Senans. Ledoux worked for the state before the revolution of 1789 that put an end to Marie-Antoinette's way of life – and indeed in 1794 her life itself, as well as that of her architect Richard Mique. During this time Ledoux was responsible for the toll houses that controlled the entry of goods into Paris and marked the edges of the city. Here, farmers who wanted to reach the city's markets had to pay a tax to be allowed through. Ledoux called them 'propylées' – propylaea, like the gateway building of the Athenian acropolis – but everyone else called them 'barrières', because they saw them as blocking the way, rather than being openings to the city.

There were fifty-seven of these gateways, and Ledoux designed pavilions to accompany forty-seven of them. Most of these were demolished after the revolution because they were a symbol of the oppressive presence of the old state, in which the aristocracy was exempt from taxation, but where everyone else paid a substantial levy to the state. One of the two pavilions to survive is the rotunda at the Porte de Saint Martin (now known as the Rotonde Stalingrad, because it is on the Place de la Bataille de Stalingrad in modern Paris – *see* Fig. 85). Here we can see the kind of architectural language that Ledoux developed: classical in its derivation, but simplified to pure geometric shapes – mainly circles and squares – cut in solid stone.

These were not large buildings, but they had assertive monumentality, carrying with them the authority of the state and contrasting with the buildings around them, which used more ephemeral construction techniques, and which – here on the edge of the city – would have had relatively modest status. No other eighteenth-century buildings survive in the area.

Ledoux's saltworks – his largest and most complex project – was built in the middle of a forest far from Paris, and escaped destruction. It used the same sort of geometric classicism as the barrières, but

Fig. 85 Claude-Nicolas Ledoux, Barrière Saint-Martin (1784–88).

was supplemented with elements of what Ledoux called 'architecture parlante' – direct, representational imagery drawn from the use of the building.

The saltworks produced salt from underground caves. Rather than mining it in blocks, the salt was brought to the surface by pumping water down and dissolving the salt. Once in solution the water could be evaporated off to produce a residue of salt crystals. In a hotter climate the saline solution could be left in the open air for the sun to do the work, but here in east-central France the process was helped along by burning wood. It was easier to transport the saltwater than the wood, so it was brought some 16km in pipes to the saltworks, close to the forest, where heat was applied and the crystals were produced.

The entrance to the saltworks is a grand classical propyleon with six sturdy Doric columns supporting an entablature. The spacing of the columns follows the example of the propyleon of the acropolis at Athens, with a wider space at the centre, where there is the opening for the portal – an extra triglyph plus metope in the frieze above. Behind the row of columns there is an arrangement of very roughly hewn boulders, which looks like a cave. It is reminiscent of the underground caverns from which the salt came.

In the low-key blocks that flank the entrance, the walls are blank except for three small windows on each side. They don't look like windows. The window surround is sculpted to look like the end of a pipe, half full of some sort of sediment that is dripping from the end of the pipe, forming stalactite-like shapes. It is as though these are pipes of saltwater, building up a deposit of crystals over time. From the inside one sees a semi-circular window. From the outside there is a sculptural decoration that explains something about the function of the building.

Another remarkable tour-de-force here is the portico of the director's house (Fig. 86). The whole

Fig. 86 Claude-Nicolas Ledoux, Director's house, at the Royal Saltworks, Arc-et-Senans (1774–79).

saltworks is laid out on a semi-circular plan. It might have grown to be a full circle had the future taken a different course. The geometry of the layout is striking and emphatic, and the director's house is right at the centre, where it seems to see, as well as control, everything that is going on in the complex.

The gateway building brings one into the big semi-circular space with the director's house directly opposite. Its façade presents an even more imposing Doric portico, again with six columns, but these are evenly spaced, and the shafts alternate with prismatic cuboid blocks of stone that seem to show the blocks from which the shafts might have been carved. They are a development in a tradition of rusticated columns.

It was ancient practice to carve columns roughly at the quarry before transporting them to the building – this avoided having to carry an excessive extra weight of stone that would be thrown away once it reached its destination. However, it was a good idea to finish the stones in situ, both to protect the surfaces from damage on the journey and to ensure the perfect alignment of stone surfaces in the finished building. For example, during the Renaissance we find Giulio Romano using columns with stone that was carved to look rough (rusticated); the idea might have come from seeing a ruin of an incomplete Roman building, or from the Porto Maggiore in Rome, where the rough surfaces seem to be the result of decay.

It became part of the repertoire of Renaissance classicism to use rusticated columns with bands of rough masonry, but here at Arc-et-Senans the bands are not rough, but suggest a great mass of stone, some of which has been carved away to reveal the columns. It suggests a rethinking of architecture from primary forms, and the effect is powerful to the point of being overbearing.

After the revolution, Ledoux's work dried up. He was associated too closely with the old state. Deprived of actual building projects, he continued to design, but in a way that was increasingly removed from practicality. He lived until 1806, and in old age collected and published his designs as a book – a copy of which found its way to Sir John Soane in London, who was a subscriber. In that collection Ledoux continued to explore the possibilities of geometry and the symbolism of primary shapes, but with no possibility of the buildings being constructed, he could let his imagination loose. For example there is a design for a cemetery, based on large circular forms in plan and in section. However, it is in the drawing that is labelled as an elevation that the symbolism is made explicit. It is not a drawing that could be issued to a builder, but is a view of planets circling one another in space.

Another round building – spherical, with stepped bridges going across an excavated square pit to relatively conventional classical doorways – is labelled as a house for the agricultural guards, by which he means herdsmen. The herdsmen are depicted in the foreground (Fig. 87). A 'troupeau' (masculine) is a herd of animals in French, while a 'troupe' (feminine) is a troop of soldiers.

As a practical commission there would have been problems with this building. It would not have been buildable in materials that were available at the time, and the herdsmen would never have been able to find the money to finance such a monumental undertaking – even after the revolution. Throughout the collection, which purports to show designs for monuments in an ideal town, people of modest social rank are given grandiose accommodation. It is as if the revolution has turned everything upside down and made princes of us all – though of course in the real world the declaration that all citizens had equal rights did not bring with it an equality of income.

There is perhaps some dark facetious humour in these proposed buildings. It is certainly there in the most notorious of the designs – a monumental brothel, in a correct and austere classical style, but presented in plan it has the form of an erect phallus. Again this has no plausibility as a building that might be in any town, anywhere, given the function of the building and the cost of executing something so monumental.

Fig. 87 Claude-Nicolas Ledoux, herdsmen's house (published 1804).

Meanwhile in Britain and The USA

In protestant Britain post-Baroque classicism began early, with architects showing more interest in the books of Palladio than in anything promoted by the Counter Reformation. English baroque could be theatrical and lively, and there was a continuing interest is bringing off Gothic effects using a classical vocabulary of forms. Sir Christopher Wren's office designed many city churches after the Great Fire of London to replace the lost medieval churches. They piled up classical ornament to make Gothic-style spires and pinnacles. Sir John Vanbrugh was responsible for some of the grandest country palaces in England, such as Castle Howard and Blenheim Palace, which cultivated what Vanbrugh liked to call 'a castle air' within a classical idiom, so there are towers and pinnacles and lively romantic silhouettes to his buildings (Fig. 88).

That kind of exuberance was reined in by the people who looked to Palladio as their authority, especially Lord Burlington, whose influence was perhaps most widely felt when it came to the design of grand country houses – which would have been called villas or palaces had they been built in Italy. The project of steering taste away from the baroque towards Palladio was supported by the publication of the three folio volumes of *Vitruvius Britannicus* (1715–25) by Colen Campbell (1676–1729), whom Burlington promoted. The term 'baroque' was not then in use for architecture, but he acknowledges the 'restorers of architecture' – which is to say the Renaissance architects who brought Roman architecture back into currency, Bramante heading his list – and praises Palladio's works above all. On the other hand he finds the work of Bernini to be 'affected and licentious', and Borromini unleashes extraordinary hostility:

> How wildly extravagant are the designs of Borromini, who has endeavoured to debauch mankind with his odd and chimerical beauties, where the parts are without proportion, solids without their true bearing, heaps of materials without strength, excessive ornaments without grace, and the whole without symmetry?
>
> (from Colen Campbell's Introduction to
> volume 1 of *Vitruvius Britannicus*)

Fig. 88 Sir John Vanbrugh, Castle Howard, York (1699–1712).

This is informed by the same impulse as Laugier's will to simplify architecture, but instead of reaching for the primitive to ground his speculations, Campbell reaches for Palladio, and his examples are all drawn from British architecture that has been informed by classical taste, opening with Wren's Saint Paul's Cathedral – so he evidently saw Wren as being in the same tradition of design as Palladio, and free from the barbarities of Bernini and Borromini. In more recent discussion these designers tend to be put in different categories, and eighteenth-century Palladianism is seen as something quite distinct from Wren's baroque and from the later neoclassicism, but they are categories that became defined in a later age. In the eighteenth century the reverence for Palladio in Britain, especially in Burlington's circle, is less evident in continental Europe, but it is to be found with Thomas Jefferson, both at home at Monticello (1768) and in his design for the University of Virginia (1819).

It is at the university that Jefferson's ideas about architecture are most developed, with a set of ten pavilions arranged along a lawn – five on each side, with a library in the general form of the Pantheon on axis closing the vista (Fig. 89). Jefferson had travelled in Europe and knew his Palladio. The pavilions are linked by an open colonnade of Tuscan columns that, proportionally speaking, are set further apart than they would be in an ancient temple. Their regular rhythm is usually, but not always, broken when the colonnade reaches a pavilion. The pavilions are given individual treatments, using different column types and sizes – some of them becoming imposing with a giant order – and the columns going up through two storeys, the whole height of the building. In others the low colonnade marches through uninterrupted, but engaged with the building. There is a general idea of symmetry, but it is not rigidly applied, so there is a feeling of flexibility within the discipline that has been set up.

Fig. 89 Thomas Jefferson, University of Virginia, Charlottesville (1819–25). This illustration shows most prominently Pavilion III, with Corinthian columns, engaging with the covered walkway that uses much smaller Tuscan columns.

Greek Models

When architects look to Palladio and his contemporaries for their idea of what architecture should be, then in the art-history world they tend to be called Palladian, even if the influence is not very precise. Any eighteenth-century house with regular windows and a central portico might be called Palladian. The term 'neoclassical' tends to be used when there is a trace of influence from Greek archaeology, or speculation about the more primitive origins of architecture, such as we have seen with Ledoux. A house such as The Grange in Hampshire shows this influence. In 1804 William Wilkins (1778–1839) was engaged to remodel the house. He had travelled in Greece and the parts of modern Turkey that had been Greek in ancient times, and would publish *The Antiquities of Magna Graecia* (1807). The house was faced in stone, given a Doric frieze, and at one end a Doric portico six columns wide accurately based on the temple of Hephaistos that looks out across the agora at Athens – a temple that Wilkins knew as the Thission.

A contemporary in Northumberland, Sir Charles Monck (1779–1867), visited Athens for his honeymoon in 1804–1806 (his first child was born there); on his return he designed Belsay Hall, which shows the influence of his careful measurement of ancient monuments (Fig. 90). There is a severe top-lit central hall with two storeys of fluted columns, as in an ancient temple; the lower columns are Ionic. The entrance is flanked by two giant Doric columns, which are more than just tokens because they are set at the top of three inconveniently tall steps – as was normal in an ancient Doric temple – and below a Doric frieze that runs right round the building, as do the steps.

Fig. 90 Sir Charles Monck, Belsay Hall, Northumberland (1810–17).

The Greek temples usually had three steps running all the way round, and they were proportioned to the size of the columns, not to the size that was convenient for humans to use – so a large temple such as the Parthenon had large steps, and where processions entered the building there was a ramp. At Belsay the columns are shorter than the Parthenon's and the steps are not so high, and can be used. They are about the height of two normal steps, so they are not suitable for dignified formal use. At the main entrance the modern visitor has the assistance of a flight of temporary-looking timber steps set over the stone ones, and presumably something comparable was always in place there.

The house is based on a square plan, and all the principal rooms have tall sash windows that come down to the floor and can be raised to above head height – so from every room on the ground floor there is access to the garden, down the three large steps. This makes the house feel unusually open to the outside. It does not have a peristyle as do the ancient Greek temples, but it is, in its way, open. Perhaps surprisingly it almost conforms to Laugier's rules about building – broken only by its few pilasters. The two Doric columns at the entrance are fully modelled, and the house becomes an authoritative monument that has much in common with Ledoux's prismatic shapes, but here they are softened by decorative detail modelled with precision on ancient Athenian sources.

Johann-Joachim Winckelmann

The story of Greek archaeology is traced back to Johann-Joachim Winkelmann (1717–1768), who worked mainly at the Vatican, where there was the largest collection of classical sculptures. Winckelmann supposed some of them at least to be Greek, and set about classifying them so as to arrive at a sense of how ancient art had developed through the centuries. We now think that the statues he thought were Greek were actually Roman copies in stone of Greek bronzes, so in some respects his scholarship has been superseded, but he tried to explain why it was that Greek sculpture was better than any other – and found it to be, because the Greek citizens including the sculptors had freedom, which shaped and elevated their thoughts.

Winckelmann's *History of Ancient Art* was published in 1764 and had huge influence across Europe. In 1768 he was invited to Vienna to meet the Empress Maria Theresa, but he was murdered in a hotel in Trieste on his way back to Rome. An effect of Winckelmann's writing was to make ancient Greek sculpture more desirable than any other, and expeditions set out to find it. Stuart and Revett's *The Antiquities of Athens* has been mentioned above, and the Society of Dilettanti that published it also commissioned *Specimens of Ancient Sculpture* (1809), showing sculptures that belonged to its members, especially Charles Townley, who sold his collection of ancient statues – mainly Roman – to the fairly new British Museum. Winckelmann had identified one of them – two boys playing knucklebones – as a work by Praxiteles, a Greek sculptor of the time just before Alexander the Great; however, his attribution is no longer accepted.

Townley's collection was upstaged by the arrival in London of the sculptures from the Parthenon from 1802, brought by Lord Elgin, the British ambassador to the Ottoman Empire, in circumstances that remain controversial. The statues remained Elgin's property until they were bought by the British state in 1816 for the British Museum. In 1821 the Louvre acquired its spectacular Greek treasure, the Winged Victory of Samothrace. Germany established a special relationship with Greece, and not only by collecting statuary: in 1807 Ludwig I of Bavaria had the idea for

a German Valhalla, which would give people from the various German states common cause by celebrating their heroes. The idea was that it would help to bring about a united German nation, something that did eventually happen in 1871, when Berlin, the capital of Prussia, became the national capital. The Valhalla would take the form of the Parthenon.

Also in 1807 Hegel's *Phenomenology of Spirit* was published, which argued that the spirit that had made ancient Greece great was active in the German world and German language of his day – and I would like to see Ludwig's project taking shape in the shadow of Georg Hegel's sense of German destiny. It is not likely that Ludwig read Hegel, but he might nevertheless have heard about his ideas. There was an important readership that found him plausible. In 1807 Hegel was at the University of Jena, and saw Napoleon (whom he called 'the world-soul on horseback') when he took the city. Hegel went on to be the Professor of Philosophy at the University of Berlin from 1818.

The high estimation of Greek art and philosophy, and the feeling of kinship and destiny, meant that in western Europe there was wide sympathy for the cause of Greek independence. The Byzantine Empire was absorbed into the Ottoman Empire after 1453 (the Fall of Constantinople). A limited part of it achieved independence in 1821 and adopted Nafplio as its capital, which had been used as an administrative centre for the region by the Ottomans. The new nation established a monarchy and chose one of Ludwig's sons, Otto (Greek sources tend to use Otho) to be the first King of Greece. He was sworn in in 1832, by which time the construction of his father's Valhalla was well under way (Fig. 91).

In 1834 Athens was adopted as the capital of Greece because of the fame of its monuments in the west. Karl Friedrich Schinkel (1781–1841), the most brilliant Prussian architect, drew up a design for the royal palace, placing it on the Acropolis and incorporating the original Parthenon in it. That idea was never realised, but it makes clear how strongly the Greek and German ideals were bonded at that time. Some of the most striking neoclassical buildings in

Fig. 91 Leo von Klenze, Valhalla, Regensburg (1830–42).

Athens are by Schinkel's former apprentice Theophil Hansen (1813–1891), who came from Denmark and designed institutional buildings that included polychromy, as excavations suggested that it had been used in the ancient world. His and his brother Christian's buildings convincingly show how rich, bright colours can be integrated into walls, columns and friezes without in any way undermining the dignity of the buildings or their scholarly detail (Figs 92 and 93). It is certainly known that some statues were painted in ancient times, and surviving details of buildings at, for example, Olympia preserve intricate patterns painted over the austere architectural forms.

The sentiments that were stirred up by Greek nationalism and independence were not confined to Greece. The Valhalla had a nationalist purpose, trying to inspire into existence a nation that did not exist, cohering around the shared German language. In Scotland there was a desire for a national monument, and it seemed appropriate to rebuild the Parthenon

there also (Fig. 94). The modern nation of Greece does not have boundaries that match those of an ancient nation, but it finds coherence through language, and takes inspiration from its ancient culture, which it shares with the world.

Changes in the Conception of the Neoclssical

What becomes clear when we look at the neoclassical versions of antique temples is that they are no longer conceived in the same way as the ancient versions. The copying might be exact in its detail, but there are different concerns, especially for the scenic value of the building. If we take the Valhalla, for example, it is positioned not so as to face an altar or the dawn, and there is no question of carrying out any sacrifices here. The building is oriented so as to address its setting in a good way. It is at a bend in the river,

Fig. 92 Theophil Hansen, Athens Academy (1859–87).

Fig. 93 Christian Hansen, Athens University (1839–64). Detail of a painted frieze. The frieze on the cella of the Parthenon would have been seen like this between columns, and it, too, was painted, maybe colourfully.

Fig. 94 Charles Robert Cockerell and William Henry Playfair, National Monument of Scotland, Edinburgh (1823–9).

at the top of a steep bank and approached by stairs that are organised symmetrically. It is much more directly imposing than the original Parthenon, which can seem rather elusive because it is set back from the edge of the plateau of the Acropolis, and is most clearly seen from high ground – such as the Pnyx, which was out by the edge of the ancient city – or from the south side, which is away from the city centre. From the Agora, the Erechtheion can be seen, but not the Parthenon.

The positioning of the buildings was not governed by the vantage points of the picturesque. The German artists who showed ancient buildings also played up their picturesque value and made them into wonderful Romantic images, seeing them in a way that could never be confused with their depiction in ancient art. In the ancient world the function of the building was to appease the gods, and they were caught up with feelings of fear, apprehension, relief and thanksgiving that are not remotely evident in the modern tourist visitors to those places. The buildings of the ancient world were enlisted in the service of a new aesthetic ideal, which saw them as part of the ideal landscape – the landscape of Arcadia.

The temple at Bassae is in the real Arcadia, the region known by that name – which is not always like the Arcadian ideal, which typically has rolling countryside with trees and shade, bathed in golden light. It has come to be associated with the landscape paintings of Gaspar Poussin and Claude Lorrain, as well as with landscape gardens (particularly those of eighteenth-century England) that made use of garden pavilions in the form of temples to give points of interest in the scenery, and to provide facilities for sitting or eating. One of the best known is at Stourhead, where temples and woodland are grouped round a lake that opens up distant views.

Berlin: Its Museums and Antique Treasures

Back in Prussia the Elector of Brandenburg's collection of antique statuary was given a spectacular new setting in the building that we now know as the Altes Museum, designed by Schinkel and opened in 1830 (Fig. 95). From the outside it looks like a giant stoa, with a row of two-storey high Ionic columns along its length, eagles perched along its entablature, and naked horsemen enlivening the skyline. It is a much more complex building than is initially apparent. The principal floor for the museum displays is a storey above the entry level. It is reached by way of a pair of staircases that are behind the row of columns, but initially they were not closed off from the outside (a curtain wall of glass has been added behind the columns, which has changed this arrangement). Then on entering the enclosed part of the building one finds oneself unexpectedly in a round domed space with a coffered vault (like the Pantheon), which is where the best of the antique sculptures were put on display.

Schinkel's classicism is enlivened and leavened by inventive details that always give it touches of charm that stop it being ponderous. For example, at the Neue Wache there are Doric columns, but instead of the usual Doric frieze with metopes and triglyphs, each column has above it a female figure – a winged angel – clad in robes that are reminiscent of the billowing drapery of the figures of the winds in the Nereid monument, now in the British Museum.

The acquisition of antique treasures did not stop with the completion of the museum. The largest and most important of them was excavated by a German team in the 1880s: the Pergamon altar (Fig. 5, *see* Chapter 1). It was installed in Berlin in a purpose-built museum in 1910. The site of ancient

Fig. 95 Karl Friedrich Schinkel, Altesmuseum, Berlin (1825–30).

Pergamon was part of the Greek world in ancient times, but in the modern world it is in Turkey, and the arrangements for the altar's removal were made with the Ottoman government. Excavations that have been conducted in modern Greece have either stayed at their sites, or have been removed to Athens, so there are spectacular museums at, for example, Olympia (carried out by a joint German and Greek team) and Delphi (French and Greek). The last important excavation to be carried out under Ottoman rule was at Bassae, which was an Anglo-German team; most of the surviving sculptures are in the British Museum, where they were installed while the price for Lord Elgin's hoard was still being discussed.

The British Museum

Sir Robert Smirke

The architect Charles Cockerell (1788–1863) was involved with the excavation at Bassae, and made use of the distinctive capital from the inside of the temple on the outside of the Ashmolean Museum (1839–1845). The British Museum was relocated to a new building by Sir Robert Smirke (1780–1867), the construction of which started in 1823. It has a peripteron of fully modelled freestanding columns – a huge extravagance – a giant order modelled on that of the temple of Athena Polias at Priene (in modern Turkey) and the subject of a study published by the Society of Dilettanti in 1811.

It is an imposing façade that seems strangely placed as it is approached by small streets in Bloomsbury. It was under construction at the same time as William Wilkins' design for the National Gallery in Trafalgar Square, which seems rather under-scaled for its position. Had they occupied each other's sites, both places would have been quite different. The National Gallery would have settled into Bloomsbury in a very satisfactory way, but the British Museum on the then-new Trafalgar Square would have turned the square into a place of overbearingly triumphant imperialism.

Smirke was in fact responsible for the design of the building that is now Canada House, on the west side of Trafalgar Square – the first building to go up after the demolition of the warren of criminal-infested buildings, where there is now open space. It was built from 1824 as a club house at one end and for the Royal College of Physicians' headquarters at the other. It is a sensible building, with relatively few columns – they are fully modelled at each end of the building, making for good, well-marked entrances – and a simple moulding goes round to suggest a continuous entablature, even when it is going along a plain wall. Smirke's great contribution to the history of building was in controlling costs – making estimates that could be depended upon (unlike such contemporaries as John Nash, who was known to ruin clients). In fact Smirke pioneered the profession of quantity surveying.

Sir John Soane

As a student Smirke very briefly worked in the office of Sir John Soane (1753–1837), but they did not get on. Soane probably counts as the major neoclassical architect in Britain, partly because of his erudition and inventiveness, but also because he had what turned out to be one of the most important commissions of the age. He was the architect for the Bank of England during the Napoleonic wars, when taxation was high and the landowning classes put their private building projects on hold until they felt more prosperous. The bank, which was financing the wars, did well out of them, and Soane's great project – executed piecemeal over many years – was to renew the whole of the bank's site at the heart of the City of London.

His design set up a screen wall round the edge of the site, for security. It is articulated with columns, blind windows and niches, but no openings except at the secure entrances. There were courtyards that gave illumination to some of the smaller offices, but the great banking halls were lit from clerestory windows and lanterns, so there was a solemn cathedral-like atmosphere to the vaults. It was in effect a single-storey building, though some of the smaller offices doubled up.

We have access to Soane's imagination to a greater extent than any of his contemporaries, because he set out his ideas in a series of lectures for students at the Royal Academy, and because he left his house to the nation at his death; the house was extraordinarily well stocked as a museum and library, with models of buildings, paintings, drawings and sculptures, including an Egyptian sarcophagus. One strand of his thought is a primitivism informed by Laugier – and by others. He regularly employed Joseph Gandy as a watercolorist to illustrate his designs and ideas, and one of his paintings shows beavers building a dam and an orang-utan making a house – this inspired by the speculations about evolution by Lord Monboddo. Soane also had copies of William Stukeley's works, speculating about Druids and their places of worship – including the stone circle at Avebury, but also including groves of trees, which would link with Laugier's speculations about the origins of cathedrals.

At Dulwich College picture gallery Soane designed the first purpose-built art gallery that was from the outset open to the public. It incorporates a mausoleum with the mummified remains of the donors. It is a brick building with square brick columns in a primitive mode, giving this very spare, simple building, which was in the countryside when it was built, monumental dignity through its suggestions of classicism, while still using materials and a level of finish that are appropriate to the setting.

The Church of Sainte Geneviève

Going back to the baroque architecture world in which Laugier's essay was written, when Laugier looked around him he disapproved of almost every new building he saw. The only one that he praised was the new church of Sainte Geneviève in Paris, commissioned by Louis XV who had been praying to the saint – the patron saint of Paris – when he had an illness, and promised her that if he recovered he would build a new church in which her bones might be placed (Fig. 96).

The building was designed by Jacques-Germain Soufflot (1713–1780), who studied in Rome and learnt particularly from the example of Bramante. The church is on a hill – a relatively low hill, but enough to give the building prominence in the city. Its plan was a Greek cross with a dome at the centre, as Bramante and Michelangelo intended for Saint Peter's, but here, as there, the nave stretched to be longer. The columns and entablatures are treated as distinct elements and are not overlaid with ornament or inflected by any baroque gestures. A frieze of garlands remembering those of the Ara Pacis in Rome continues round the outside of the building at the level of the capitals, and inside there is a richly decorated entablature above the columns; the overall clean lines are therefore enriched with decoration that is kept within the bounds of the architectural lines (Fig. 97). Soufflot himself died before the building was completed, and before the upheavals that tore apart the society he knew.

Soufflot was associated with the aristocracy through the Marquis de Marigny, Abel-François Poisson de Vandières (1751–1781), whose older sister was Madame de Pompadour, the most powerful of Louis XV's mistresses. Louis put the eighteen-year-old Poisson de Vandières in charge of all the royal building and garden projects. Poisson de Vandières' education for the role took him on a Grand Tour to Rome between 1749 and 1751. Soufflot was his companion and guide, and Poisson de Vandières put him in charge of the royal buildings in Paris. Madame de Pompadour commissioned the Élysée Palace, which is now the official residence of the French presidents, and Soufflot designed a *hôtel particulier* – a palace – for her brother, just across the road from it: the Hôtel de Marigny.

In the 1790s, after the revolution, Saint Geneviève's bones were destroyed, as happened in many other places as religious buildings were desacralised and made into temples of reason, or variations on that

Fig. 96 Jacques-Germain Soufflot, Sainte Geneviève, later the Panthéon (1755 onwards).

Fig. 97 Jacques-Germain Soufflot, detail of Panthéon garlands – compare with Fig. 12 (chapter 2).

theme. Saint Geneviève's church was turned into a place for the burial and memorialisation of the illustrious dead, and renamed the Panthéon after the former temple church in Rome, which had been used in that way since the sixteenth century (Raphael is buried there). The lower windows of the Parisian Panthéon were blocked up to improve the building's structural stability, and now the interior is illuminated only from clerestory windows. The mood is, of course, sepulchral.

Napoleon's Architects

The high point for French neoclassicism was under Napoleon, who assumed office as First Consul in 1799 and as Emperor in 1804. He conquered Venice in 1797 and declared himself King of Italy in 1805 – assuming a title that had last been used in the sixteenth century by Holy Roman Emperors.

In 1806 he commissioned the architects Percier and Fontaine to build a triumphal arch in the Place du Carrousel to support and display the four brass horses looted from San Marco in Venice – which Venice had looted from Constantinople in 1204. As a trophy they laid claim to a direct line of succession to the most splendid imperial past. The arch also acted as a gateway to the Tuileries palace. A large square in front of it was used for military display manoeuvres involving troops and their horses wheeling round in formation: these displays were called 'carrousels', deriving from an Italian word for a play-battle. The fairground roundabouts that we call 'carrousels' take their name from this display. Having the horses from Constantinople preside over it makes perfect iconographic sense, just as it had made sense to have them watch over the chariot races at the hippodrome. The originals are now kept in museum conditions in Venice, and both the Arc du Carrousel and San Marco's façade have replicas, which give the correct architectural effect.

The more famous and larger Arc de Triomphe on the Champs Elysées is on the same axis as the Arc du Carrousel, and it was commissioned at the same time, but took much longer to complete. It was designed by Jean Chalgrin (1739–1811), and then the supervision of the construction was taken over by Jean-Nicolas Huyot (1780–1840) after Chalgrin's death. The work was suspended with Napoleon's departure from office in 1814 and through the duration of the Bourbon Restoration, which saw – for a while – the return of the line of monarchs from before the revolution.

Percier and Fontaine were Napoleon's favourite architects. Charles Percier (1764–1838) and Pierre-François-Léonard Fontaine (1762–1853) met as students in the atelier of Antoine-François Peyre, and both studied in Rome. They set up practice together, lived together and are buried together at the Père Lachaise cemetery. Under Napoleon they designed interiors for many palaces, including the Louvre and the Tuileries, and the Rue de Rivoli, with its long arcade that still stretches along the length of the modern Louvre and the Tuileries gardens (Fig. 98). Their influence shaped the architectural taste of the establishment, until Napoleon's downfall. Thereafter they had fewer commissions, but their influence continued through a very successful atelier at the École des Beaux Arts, run under Percier's name; the school produced many successful graduates.

Their style is richly decorated and as sumptuous as anything baroque, but the ornamentation is always kept within the borders established by the lines of apparent structure. Columns can be seen very cleanly to be supporting entablatures, which run through uninterrupted as straight lines. This discipline is maintained while the surfaces above and below and framed by the orders can be richly sculpted. The scale of operations is also larger than had been seen before since the building of Versailles. Under Napoleon the military example of Roman conquests comes to the fore in the neoclassicism of his reign, for example with the triumphal arches. There was also a grand temple of military glory that became the Church of the Madeleine. It was not completed until later, but its grand conception is completely neoclassical, informed by Greek and Roman models.

Fig. 98 Charles Percier and Pierre François Léonard Fontaine, Louvre, Paris (they were involved with the Louvre for decades, but this room dates from about 1812).

The general form of the church is that of a Roman temple, with a flight of steps up to the entrance. However, unlike Roman temples, but like Greek ones, there is a peripteron of fully modelled columns going all the way round. It is 108 metres long and its columns are 20 metres high. (For comparison the Parthenon is 73 metres long and its columns 10.5 metres high.) The interior is vaulted in a distinctly late Roman or Byzantine manner, with three coffered domes on pendentives covering the nave, each with an oculus in the top (as at the Pantheon in Rome), which are the main source of natural light for the building. The architect was Pierre-Alexandre Vignon (1763–1828), who won the commission in competition – Napoleon selected this design, against the advice of his jury (Fig. 99).

Construction began in 1808, but the building remained incomplete at Vignon's death; it was eventually finished in 1842. The orientation of the church is liturgically unconventional as the main altar is not

Fig. 99 Pierre-Alexandre Vignon, La Madeleine, Paris (1807–28).

in the east but in the north end of the building. The orientation is determined entirely by considerations of urbanism. The building is aligned axially with the obelisk in the Place de la Concorde – a trophy from Luxor – and with the National Assembly across the river. Looking from the obelisk one can see the gilded dome of the Invalides – built in the time of Louis XIV by Jules Hardouin-Mansart (1646–1708) at the military academy (Fig. 73, *see* Chapter 6). Napoleon's body is kept there on a catafalque.

One extraordinary building from the Restoration came Percier and Fontaine's way – the Expiatory Chapel (Fig. 100). It is a small but elaborately set up chapel marking the place where the bodies of Louis XVI and Marie-Antoinette were buried after their execution until they were taken to be reburied in the traditional royal burial place, the basilica of Saint Denis. It is in a city square, now known as the Square Louis XVI, but it does not sit in alignment with the surrounding buildings. Its orientation on

Fig. 100 Charles Percier and Pierre François Léonard Fontaine, Chapelle Expiatoire, Paris (1816–26).

an east–west axis suggests that it has its mind on higher things than the immediate surroundings, but unexpectedly its altar is at the west, beneath a coffered dome with statues of the king and queen looking pious. The east door is approached along an avenue of white rose bushes, and there is a surrounding cloister with vaults and memorials to other people who were buried here.

In Conclusion

The neoclassical impulse in architecture looks for propriety rather than exuberance. For its detractors it is stale and repetitive. For its advocates it is correct. The best of it finds real inspiration in adherence to the rules, and any architectural style can become dull when it is formulaic. The key point to be made here is that neoclassicism does not designate a period in architectural history. In a way the early Renaissance architecture was neoclassical, and ancient historians sometimes call it just that. It is moved by many of the same impulses as the Palladianism of eighteenth-century England, but the term neoclassical is not used for that. It is clearest when it means post-baroque classicism, as that shows the necessary repudiation of the baroque ideals of plasticity and animation in favour of discipline and stability.

But as we have seen, the baroque did not suddenly die out, and it continued to be used confidently through the nineteenth century and beyond. Neoclassicism, with its clear geometries and sober character, also continued to be used right through the twentieth century.

Chapter Eight

Eclectic Classicism

Classicism with Alternatives

By the end of the nineteenth century, everybody knew that there were high-status alternatives to classicism, even if they did not adopt them. Eugène Viollet-le-Duc (1814–1879) had been calling for a new nineteenth-century architecture that responded to the new building material of iron in the way the medieval masons had responded to stone – exploring the structural possibilities in a rational and expressive way. The nineteenth century had seen the revival of Gothic in some high-status buildings (for example, the Palace of Westminster in London), and Viollet-le-Duc's promptings nudged architects into inventing Art Nouveau, perhaps Art Deco, and then the modernism that came to be known as the International Style, or the Modern Movement. These alternatives did not extinguish the building of classical architecture, though there are certainly occasions when classical buildings seem to be doing no more than repeating well-tried patterns, and the sense of exploration and inventiveness is more evident elsewhere.

Neoclassicism in Washington DC

The memorial for Abraham Lincoln that terminates the long axis of the National Mall in Washington DC is an impressively monumental exercise in sober neoclassicism, dating from the early years of the twentieth century. It was designed by Henry Bacon (1866–1924) who had previously been employed by McKim, Mead, White – an architectural firm that produced many refined classical buildings (Fig. 101). Building work started in 1914 and was finished by 1922 when the building was inaugurated. It is closely modelled on a Doric temple, and at first glance looks much like the Parthenon. However, the slight

Fig. 101 Henry Bacon, Lincoln Memorial, Washington DC (1914–22).

differences are telling. There are eight columns across the short sides of both buildings, but the Parthenon has seventeen along the long sides while the Lincoln Memorial has twelve. The key difference is that it is an even number of columns, so on the central axis of the building there is a space, not a column. That is where the entrance is.

The Parthenon has two portals, and they are both in the short sides of the building, one looking east to the altar, the other west. Here at the Lincoln Memorial there is just one entrance and it is in the long side of the building, which faces east. There is a colossal statue of Abraham Lincoln, just like a cult statue of an ancient god, but instead of looking out east to an altar where sacrifices would be made, he looks east along the axis of the mall to the great dome of the Capitol building, 3.7 kilometres away.

The ancient Doric temple with an entrance in the long side is the temple at Bassae. (There seem to have been other temples with this arrangement in the region, so it may have been a local temple type.) There, however, the entrance is not placed centrally. There are fifteen columns on the long side of the temple and six on the short sides – so the building is a little longer than the usual proportion – normally thirteen would be expected on the long side, for six across the pedimented ends. This side entrance is positioned with five columns on one side of it and ten on the other.

Going back to the Lincoln Memorial: instead of the expected three giant steps all the way round the temple, making a stepped plinth (a stylobate), there are only steps on the entrance side of the building, and going up a taller-than-expected plinth with steps that are the right size for walking up – as in a Roman temple such as the Maison Carrée at Nîmes (*see* Fig. 14, Chapter 2). The roof is concealed behind a tall parapet, and there is no sloping pediment at either end of the building. The columns are 13.4 metres high, significantly larger than those of the Parthenon (which are 10 metres), but smaller than the Madeleine in Paris – this is not an exercise in gigantism. The scale is imposing, but in its setting it is not overbearing.

This monument is on low, fairly flat ground, not raised up above the city on an acropolis, so the tall plinth raises the set-apart interior above the throng, if there is a throng. The whole mall has the character of a sanctuary, and there are elements of the set-up that an ancient Greek would find familiar, but others would be left puzzling – in particular the function of the building, which lacks an altar and so could not function in the expected way. What is the role of the statue, if it cannot act as a god? The scale of the ensemble takes its cue from the great days of imperial Rome, or from the palace at Versailles.

Another memorial is on the same axis: the Washington Monument, which takes the form of an obelisk, but unlike the Roman and French obelisks it was not a monolith looted from Egypt, but a building in the form of an obelisk – the tallest building in the world from 1884 until the construction of the Eiffel Tower in 1889. The alignment of the monument with the Capitol on an axis marked by an obelisk repeats the alignment of the Madeleine with the Assemblée Nationale across the obelisk in Paris.

The whole city of Washington DC, including the axis of the National Mall, was laid out by a French military engineer, Pierre-Charles l'Enfant (1754–1825), whose father had painted battle scenes for Louis XV – so the example of the aligned vistas of Versailles and Paris was part of his conception of the city. That vision was developed over later generations with buildings that have often seemed to be evoking imperial grandeur. The tone is set by the Capitol itself, with its grandiose dome dating from 1855 and constructed by 1866. Like the dome of Saint Peter's in Rome and Saint Paul's in London, the dome is raised up high above the main building and is there principally for its monumental effect, not for the sake of the interior space. It was designed by Thomas Ustick Walter (1804–87) and built in cast iron – not that one would guess. Its finish matches the white stone of the building to which it was added. Its appearance owes a great deal to the architects of the baroque, but the constructional method owes them nothing.

The international classicism has several details such as corn-cob capitals, which in places are a substitute for Corinthian ones, using the indigenous crop instead of the Greek acanthus. Like the Thanksgiving feast in which corn plays a part, this brings a local element into the grand narrative of the imperial tradition going back to Rome, and does so in just the way that was done in ancient Rome (for example with the capitals inside the temple of Mars Ultor, *see* Fig. 19, Chapter 2).

John Russell Pope's Neoclassicism

One of its neighbours is the National Gallery of Art, which was designed in 1930 by John Russell Pope (1874–1937). He studied in New York and Rome, and at the École des Beaux Arts in Paris, and brought a suave elegance to combinations of classical precedents in his designs. Modern construction methods allowed him greater flexibility than the ancients had, so his interior spaces can flow into one another in ways that make them feel modern.

Also, although there have been some rearrangements, the function of his buildings is often the same now as when they were built, which is never the case with buildings from the ancient world. His design for the National Gallery – now known as the West Building, because an extension was built to the east of it – has Ionic porticoes with eight columns (octastyle) on two sides of the building. One of them is approached by a flight of steps up to the principal floor from the National Mall, and you enter the building between the columns. On the other side the entrance is at pavement level, below the principal floor, and the doors are in the 'basement' level, below the columns. There is a coffered dome, modelled on the Pantheon, between the two porticoes, making a grand lobby that turns from the axis on which one enters to the axis that runs along the length of the building and sets up a grand enfilade of rooms, including courtyards with plants, which are glazed over and open to circulation from the galleries.

Pope's authoritative neoclassicism is unfussy in its decoration, and is adapted to modern institutional needs. The sequence of internal spaces is far more complex than anything we know from the ancient world, except the great bathing establishments from imperial Rome. More often we find great monuments with one or two principal rooms that are linked by way of external spaces – a garden, sanctuary or forum. Pope also designed the domed memorial for Thomas

Fig. 102 John Russell Pope, National Gallery of Art, Washington DC (1922–41).

Jefferson, which is based on the Pantheon, but opened up with four portals that link the internal space with views of the surrounding landscape. It is positioned by a tidal basin of the Potomac River, with trees around, and the setting owes more to eighteenth-century picturesque landscapes than to the Pantheon's urban setting. The temple has been reimagined as peripteral, with a ring of Ionic columns surrounding it, as well as an octastyle portico that establishes a principal axis – along which the statue of Jefferson directs its gaze.

Pope was also responsible for the National Archive building, which is across the road from the National Gallery, and just a block along. It has an imposing presence in a city that is not short of imposing classical buildings. It is a severe cuboid block that from some angles seems almost windowless, because the windows are set behind a row of columns. The decoration is restrained, but enriches the edges of the parapet against the sky. The corners of the building are plain and severe, but a row of Corinthian columns is taken across the central part, which steps forward into a portico that uses a second row of columns, and their vigorously modelled acanthus-leaf capitals proliferate in a show of extravagance, in which every element is completely under control within an austere order. There is no missing the fact that this is a high-status building.

City Design Based on Processional Axes

It was the architects of imperial Rome who developed the idea of establishing a processional axis through monumental parts of the city. The old forum of republican Rome grew up over a long time and had no unifying design. The imperial fora, on the other hand, each had an axis of symmetry, and monuments were arranged along it. There are axes like this in the gardens at Versailles and in central Paris – the longest and most important being formalised as the Champs Élysées, connecting the Tuileries with the Arc de Triomphe – now extended to reach from the Louvre to la Défense.

There were also cross axes. In Paris one of them has been mentioned, that connects the Madeleine to the Assemblée Nationale, while another, more recent one, connects the Palais de Chaillot with the École Militaire by way of the Champs de Mars and the Eiffel Tower. It became the established practice at the École des Beaux Arts in Paris to begin a design for a building by drawing a straight line across the empty page, to establish the axis of the plan. Then the second line would be a line at right-angles to it, which would be the counter axis. Traces of this thinking are to be found in the designs of anyone who went through this training, including both l'Enfant and Pope in their designs at different scales for the city of Washington.

Neoclassicism in New Delhi

The same formula is to be found in India, where New Delhi was built from 1911 when George V of Britain laid the foundation stone. As in Washington, the new administrative capital established through monuments the visible domination of the place by an architecture of European heritage that acknowledged some elements of indigenous culture while relegating them to positions of subservience. At Delhi, for example, there is the India Gate – a triumphal arch in the grand tradition of triumphal arches that starts in Rome (Fig. 103). Like the others, this is a war memorial. On axis with this there is the ruler's palace, known as the Viceroy's House when it was built (the viceroy being the king's representative) – but since 1950 it has been Rashtrapati Bhavan, the president's palace (Fig. 104).

The British architects Sir Edwin Lutyens and Sir Herbert Baker were responsible for the designs of the important buildings, with Lutyens designing the arch and the palace. The arch has a strongly geometric character and is more abstract than triumphal arches traditionally are – without groups of statue figures on any part of it. The palace has a great dome raised up high, designed to have a greater impact

The palace and other Lutyens-designed monuments here incorporate blocky, semi-abstract sculptures of elephants as a nod to local fauna. The famous dome of the Taj Mahal comes from a different tradition – from the Islamic rulers of the Punjab – but as perhaps the most recognisable Indian monument, it is clear that the dome has a place in Indian culture, and Lutyens' attempt to find common ground between the indigenous culture and Western imperial triumphalism has made it possible to assimilate it, however unwillingly, in modern India. The Indian people paid for these buildings and built them, and they are now also used by Indian people. Something similar happened in Dublin, with grandiose classical buildings built in the eighteenth century when Ireland was under British rule, but they are now reclaimed as part of Irish heritage – the work of Irish craftsmen and architects.

In Washington the history since building the monuments has been very different, and the buildings along the national mall have not, until recently, carried any trace of the culture of the indigenous peoples. There is now the Museum of the American Indians, which gives a hint of the cultures that used to inhabit the terrain, in a building that does not conform to the prevailing classical norm, like Pope's gallery on the other side of the mall. The population of Native Americans that remains after activity that now looks genocidal is small (about 2 per cent of the total official population, when once of course it was 100 per cent). About 12.4 per cent of the population is of African–American descent – many with ancestors who were forcibly brought into the country as unpaid labourers. Another 18.7 per cent are Hispanic, some brought into the country by the Louisiana Purchase and the invasion of Mexico, as well as through more recent immigration.

The dominant neoclassicism of the capital does not include examples of the baroque, which might look more Hispanic, but is distinctively sometimes suavely buttoned up. From outside it looks like the architecture of a dominant colonial power, imposing itself on the place, but as the power is real and still

Fig. 103 India Gate, New Delhi (1931) Sir Edwin Lutyens.

Fig. 104 The Viceroy's palace (now Rashtrapati Bhavan), New Delhi (1912–29) Sir Edwin Lutyens.

from a distance than it eventually achieved, because the road along which it is approached slopes more steeply at a distance from the palace, so the view of the lower storeys is cut out. Nevertheless, because it is at the top of a hill, the palace's dome has prominence from afar, and it is a recognisably Indian dome, with the profile of the great stupa of Sanchi, an ancient Buddhist shrine.

in place, people are more likely to want to identify with the expressions of power and see stability and their own good fortune in their confident expression.

Monumental Designs for Berlin

The military triumphalism that saw the construction of monumental arches also left its trace in Berlin. The Brandenburg Gate was built in the late eighteenth century (1788–1791) by Frederick William II, King of Prussia, and was a gateway to the city as well as a triumphal arch, surmounted by a quadriga, which Napoleon removed. It was just like the one he set up later using the horses from Venice, and had exactly the same symbolism: triumphal victory, symbolised through the Roman iconography of the personification of victory riding in a chariot pulled by four horses, and embodied in a trophy of war – actual plunder.

In the twentieth century a huge triumphal arch was projected for Berlin – three times the size of the Arc de Triomphe in Paris – but events took a course that meant it was not built. A huge, heavy concrete cylinder was built in the Tempelhof district of Berlin to make sure that its foundations would work. That test structure from 1941–1942 survives and is known as the 'Schwerbelastungskörper' ('heavy load-bearing body'). Had things gone according to plan for Adolf Hitler then this arch would have been on a colossal axial route aligned with a gigantic dome. This is said to have been based on the Pantheon in Rome, and it is like it in being essentially a one-room building under a dome. It would have been an assembly hall for Nazi rallies, and it would have been the largest dome in the world – 250 metres wide, compared with the Pantheon's 43 metres. The structure would have been steel, but clad in stone to give a traditional masonry cover, and dressed with neoclassical detail.

The architect was Albert Speer (1905–1981), who was closely involved with Hitler's dreams and ambitions for rebuilding the capital city in a way that would have been crushingly monumental. There have been attempts to restore his reputation as an architect, but there is no fine judgement on show here, just absolute bombast. It helps to realise that the Roman triumphs and Napoleon's victories were just as bombastic in their day, and the scale of building kept escalating through the nineteenth and twentieth centuries as the use of steel made longer spans possible, and the mechanisation of tools and factory production methods made it possible to do more, and to do it more quickly. Le Corbusier drew attention to the fact that Haussmann remodelled Paris with many of its great boulevards using an army of workmen with pickaxes, shovels and sledgehammers. From the twentieth century the workers can be equipped with bulldozers, dynamite and wrecking balls, and things can happen fast.

We can see it perhaps most clearly in Speer's intentions for Berlin that the act of building is a form of argument – or a way of closing down argument. The victorious regime is established as a real physical presence, and opposition to it is rendered futile in the face of these overpowering physical realities. In that case the power dispersed before the largest of the monuments was realised, and many other traces of its presence have been destroyed.

Rome: Grandeur Past and Present

In Italy again the history is different. During the 1920s and 1930s under Benito Mussolini (1883–1945) there was an attempt to connect with the ancient Roman imperial past. Parts of central Rome were cleared of modern developments so that the ancient relics could be brought to light, and overseas countries were invaded and annexed for a modern Italian empire that Mussolini hoped would stretch from the west of the Mediterranean to the Middle East, taking in parts of Africa. The relation between the ancient ruins and modern politics could not have been clearer. Ancient monuments were moved so as to give good processional routes past Mussolini's palace's balcony,

Fig. 105 Giovanni Guerrini, Ernesto La Padula, and Mario Romano, Palazzo della Civiltà Italiana, EUR, Rome (1935–40).

the Arch of Constantine and the largest ruin of all, the Colosseum.

Mussolini also commissioned an extension to the city of Rome, which was originally supposed to be the site for the World Fair of 1942. It was known as the Esposizione Universale Roma – EUR – and work began on it in 1937 – but then the project was derailed by war and the exhibition never took place (Fig. 105). The site was developed for commerce and housing, and it was completed after the war so there is an architectural mix that includes the clear influence of ancient Rome in its use of axial planning, colonnades and serried rows of arches, as well as later, more conventional modernist work.

The aim under Mussolini was to express the idea that the grandeur of the Roman past belonged also in the present and future, and the buildings developed a stripped geometric version of neoclassicism that looks familiar from the paintings of Giorgio de Chirico (1888–1978).

Stockholm: Nordic Classicism

Meanwhile in Scandinavia a different version of classical architecture took shape. It was aiming to be a convincingly modern architecture and used geometric forms such as cylinders and prisms rather than decorated capitals. The thing that makes Nordic Classicism look classical is the composition of the buildings, so they would typically establish a central axis and arrange columns in a portico to mark the entrance, but they would not be Corinthian columns, but a plain geometric shape – circular or square in cross-section.

The Influence of Gunnar Asplund

The architect who is now best known from among the practitioners who designed – at least for a time – in this way is Gunnar Asplund (1885–1940). He began his career designing in a neoclassical way, but took an interest in the debates around modernity and what a modern architecture should be like, and later in his career – which was not a very long career, as he died at fifty-five – he was designing in a clearly modernist idiom.

The key building to demonstrate the change is in Gothenburg – the law courts – which he began in 1914 and completed in 1937. Asplund was extending an older building – designed by Nicodemus Tessin, dating from 1672 – in a classical style with an eclectic range of details. There is a Doric frieze with triglyphs, and Tuscan pilasters below it. Tuscan columns are like unfluted Doric columns, but they have a modelled base, whereas fully Doric columns are sliced off without modulation, so their flutes come directly into contact with the stylobate – the platform. The pilasters turn into three-quarter columns for the four-columned portico arrangement above the main entrance. These pilasters are two storeys high (giant columns), but the entrance itself uses smaller columns – four pairs of them – with arched openings between them, so they look like a Roman triumphal arch, but the paired columns look as if they come from French influence. The columns and pilasters are ranged across a straight façade, dividing it into nine regular bays, each with a window on each floor.

Asplund's extension has no explicitly classical detail, but it keeps the rhythm of the windows and bays, adding six new bays on one side of the building. The windows are not symmetrically placed within the bays, which are established by what looks like a structural frame rather than decorative pilasters. The windows are placed off-centre in the bays, but they continue the rhythm from the older building. The façade of the old building suggests that its principal rooms are on the first floor – the *piano nobile* – and the windows are taller on that level. In the extension the windows are normal height, but the first four bays have a sculptural panel above the window. They resemble the metope panels from a Doric frieze, but a much larger one than is actually on the old building.

The overall impression is of seamless continuity between the original building and its extension, and Asplund was looking for ways to find common ground between the classical and the modern – an aim that was often repudiated by the architects associated with CIAM – the international congresses of modern architecture – which did so much to establish what became known as the International Style.

Asplund also designed Stockholm's central Public Library, which is classical without any classical ornament (Fig. 106). Its formal arrangement is a large

Fig. 106 Gunnar Asplund, Stockholm Public Library (1922–28).

cylinder set in a lower square block. It was originally conceived in 1918 to have a central dome (like the British Library completed by Sydney Smirke in 1857). By the time it was finished in 1928 all the decorative classical details had been eliminated. It resembles the composition of Ledoux's Barrière Saint Martin, but on a much larger scale (*see* Fig. 85, Chapter 7, and compare Fig. 24, Chapter 3). Ledoux's work was already very geometric in its inspiration, and its classical columns were simplified and abstract. At the Stockholm library they have gone altogether, but what remains has a simple, elemental gravity. It is approached on axis up a flight of ramped steps to its monumental doorway. The door has a stone frame – an architrave – that tapers towards the top, as in a Greek temple, and that is the only decorative element in the façades beyond the thin stone coping – which does nothing to make it resemble a classical entablature.

The repetitive grids made by steel or concrete frames in modern buildings can be given proportions and a sensibility that makes one want to say they have something of the classical about them. For example, this is often said about Mies van der Rohe's buildings, which treat the I-section industrial steel column with a reverence that gives it the status of a classical order. Buildings such as Crown Hall at Illinois Institute of Technology have a regularity and symmetry that call a classical temple to mind (Fig. 107). The link here is Gottfried Semper's book, translated as *Style in the Tectonic Arts: Practical Aesthetics* (1860–1862).

The Influence of Gottfried Semper

Semper (1803–1879) was an important architect who designed major buildings in Vienna, Dresden and Zürich. They are impressive because of their

Fig. 107 Mies van der Rohe, Crown Hall, Illinois Institute of Technology (completed 1956).

size and complexity, resolving the demands of large institutions into sober classical piles. It is his writing that is significant for the development of later ideas. His way of thinking about classical architecture was, like Laugier, to refer it back to the pattern of a hut. In Semper's case it was a real hut that had come from the Caribbean and had been put on show in London at the Great Exhibition in the Crystal Palace in Hyde Park. Semper encountered it when he visited London in 1851, and it lodged in his imagination – perhaps surprisingly, for him it acted as more of an inspiration than the great greenhouse of the Crystal Palace itself, which is often taken to be a starting point for modern architecture.

Semper analysed the hut as composed of four elements: the earthwork of its base, which raised the floor from the surroundings and acted as a plinth for the other elements; the hearth, which gave a social focus; and thirdly the timber framework of columns and beams that gave the volume of the building its structure. The 'tectonic arts' in Semper's imagination were arts derived from making things – especially the frameworks that made the structure of buildings. The fourth element was the textiles that enveloped the building and made it weatherproof. In the primitive hut these might be woven slats, canvas or carpet. When they are translated into a classical building they might become stone, but when they are translated into a steel-framed building they become large sheets of glass or insulated composited panels – and they are called 'curtain walls'.

Mies van der Rohe (*see* above) took seriously the implications of expressing the constructional principles of the steel frame, and tried to put it on show, making it very clear what was structure and what was the infilling fabric. His designs could as easily spring from Laugier's invented primitive hut, but Semper's version has the advantage that the enclosing walls are part of the imaginative scheme – for Laugier, walls were always to be regretted from the point of view of aesthetics, even though he admitted that they could be necessary for a building to be useful. By comparison Semper's 'practical aesthetics' were indeed practical.

Classical Overtones in a Modernist Frame

Tectonic Frames

The classical overtones in a modernist frame are equally clear in David Chipperfield's twenty-first-century buildings on the Museuminsel in Berlin, where

Fig. 108 David Chipperfield, James Simon Museum, Museuminsel, Berlin (2004–19).

Fig. 109 Louis Perreau, central post office, Dijon (completed 1910).

he is in company with Schinkel's Altesmuseum and the Pergamon Museum (Fig. 108). The older buildings are explicitly classical, and their mood is sustained by Chipperfield's new buildings that have no classical decoration but do have a sense of the rhythms and orders of the established and authoritative context.

For a contrast we can take a look at the central post office in Dijon (1927–1932) (Fig. 109), which uses classical ornament throughout, but piled up in a way that has some overtones of the baroque and much else besides, including Art Deco. Many of its ornaments derive from classical precedents, but it doesn't really look like a classical building as there is so much about it that seems restless and inventive – but then one could say much the same with Borromini's San Carlo, and that is clearly baroque and a development in the classical tradition. The sobriety of Chipperfield's buildings in Berlin makes them seem more properly classical than the whimsical assemblage in Dijon, but they are both in their ways buildings that could not have taken shape without the classical tradition.

The Global Harbor shopping mall in Shanghai is clearly a modern building that uses modern methods of construction, and the whole ambience is clearly to be understood as a normal commercial development on a large scale (Fig. 110). Its real construction uses a steel frame, and from the point of view of tectonic expression the steel frame is what matters. It can quite clearly be inferred from what is visible, even though it is often covered up with classical ornament derived from stone construction. In fact the ornament is almost incidental to the way one perceives the building, and to link it with the tradition of architecture that goes back to ancient Europe seems a mistake. The more important and immediate link really is with more recent commercial buildings of the colonial era in Shanghai, some of them built using classical ornament – so it reclaims some symbolic status by association with the architecture of the former overlords, rather than anything more remote or historical.

Similarly there is a flourishing architectural practice of building houses that look like the inherited aristocratic houses of the eighteenth century, which do nothing to enrich the classical tradition, but allow their owners to feel that they are continuing a tradition of gentility and to lay claim to the status that goes with that tradition. In the twenty-first century

Fig. 110 Chapman Taylor, Global Harbor shopping mall, Shanghai (completed 2013).

the Château Louis XIV was built near Versailles and in the style of Louis XIV's nearby palace. It is well executed, using traditional craftsmanship, adapting the seventeenth-century appearance to the contemporary life that could go on there. There are rooms in the house that serve modern needs, also a nightclub, and a meditation room under the moat that gives underwater views of fish.

It sounds kitsch, to be dressing up such facilities in period costume, but it is so well done that it seems inappropriate to say so. Ludwig II of Bavaria had a reproduction of Versailles built on the Chiemsee in Bavaria (*see* Fig. 79, Chapter 6) and it, too, can be labelled as kitsch – but again it escapes the charge by being well done, and there is nothing trashy about it: the artworks within are original, and the work as a whole bears witness to its owner's hero-worship of Louis XIV, so it has the air of a tribute.

The Château Louis XIV is no more wrong for having been built in the twenty-first century rather than the nineteenth. Had it been built in the seventeenth century then its taste would have been pioneering, and now it is not. It is now owned by the Crown Prince of Saudi Arabia, who apparently doesn't use it, so its utility is not the point. It is a precious and finely made thing that has none of the roles of the

original Versailles palace – it is not used as a dwelling, and it is not an instrument for regulating the court and the running of the country (neither France nor Saudi Arabia). It is a private asset, apparently the most expensive house ever to have been bought. It is not open to the public – as is usual with private houses – and its purchase was shrouded in secrecy, so ostentation does not seem to be the point either.

As to its significance, from the point of view of a narrative about the developments of architectural style, it is negligible. From the point of view of a narrative about the architectural taste of the very rich, it is strong evidence that something very far removed from the avant-garde tradition can be seen as bankable. If one invests in something that is already old-fashioned then it doesn't go out of fashion because it has done that already, and with the passing of the years it will no longer be seen as a new building.

Architects usually hope that the budget for a substantial building would be spent in a way that produces something experimental and innovative, but no one has that expectation of old buildings, which come to be accepted as part of the scene. The building is future proof in terms of its cultural value, and is better adapted to contemporary life than a real seventeenth-century building would have been because it has up-to-date plumbing and electricity. The palace of Versailles had neither. Seventeenth-century French wisdom associated water with contagion – cholera and other water-borne diseases made it deadly, so it was used sparingly. Sanitation at the palace ran on chamber pots, and the body was cleaned by using dry perfumed powder rubs. By contrast there are plenty of bathrooms in the new château.

Most people most of the time do not make their dwelling a place of great innovation. They are investing their earnings in it, and need to know that the dwelling is going to work. The Château Louis XIV plays to the same instincts as a heavily mortgaged suburban house, but taken to an extreme because so much more money and status are involved.

The Timeless Beauty of Ancient Classical Architecture

One of the things we hear about ancient classical architecture is that it has a timeless beauty that represents an unchanging ideal, transcending the passage of time. That is an illusion, caused by the fact that we like to think that the people in the ancient world saw things the way we see them. The building was beautiful then, and it is beautiful now, but our culture is very different from theirs and we experience a different beauty. Martin Heidegger wrote about the Greek temple in an important philosophical essay 'The Origin of the Work of Art' in which he sees the temple as a focus in the landscape, crystallising the god's presence at the site. He makes the point that we do not know any of the ancient places as functioning temples – we know them only after their gods have fled.

We can see very clearly now that Heidegger was looking at the ancient temples through the tradition of Romantic paintings and the picturesque. He did not visit Greece until years after he wrote his essay, and knew about the appearance of the temples from paintings, prints and photographs, all of which give an impression of the building in the landscape that

is not discussed in any of the ancient writings about temples. The activity around the temple as it involved the citizens of the region would have revolved around sacrifice and eating the sacrificed carcasses. It was these sacrifices that were supposed to have a good effect: they would win the gods' support.

The making of sacrifices plays no part in the modern appreciation of the beauty of ancient temples. They are not reactivated as functioning entities. That whole belief system has passed, and we approach the buildings through our own belief system, which is profoundly different in all sorts of ways, even if from time to time there are connections. We have no accounts of ancient travellers contemplating the landscape and the building's metaphysical importance of drawing down the god to the site. This is not to say that Heidegger's writing is worthless, just that it is valuing the buildings for completely different reasons. We can be thrilled by it as a modern way to engage with the place and feel enthusiasm for it, but it is not an ancient way.

Each chapter in this book has taken a look at classical architecture that has changed. What we see when we look at classical architecture is different if we are looking at it in the fifth century BCE, in the Renaissance or in the seventeenth century. We might be looking at the same things and seeing different aspects of what is there, but actually because buildings fall down and because of the state of knowledge in different eras, we can often see that people were looking at different things. For example when Winckelmann started his great enterprise of classifying ancient sculpture, he set up a framework that is still in use, with the classic works preceded by archaic ones, and succeeded by later Hellenistic work that was often seen as accomplished but facile, without the authority of the classic statues.

However, we now know that Winckelmann's judgements were often wrong about which particular works belonged in each category. There is now more historical evidence to draw on. Winckelmann was writing about Greek sculpture but working in Rome, and knew only the Roman copies of ancient

Greek work. When it comes to buildings there are similar problems. Many of the ancient monuments in ancient Rome that are known to us now were brought to light by the excavations ordered by Mussolini in the 1930s. Earlier architects and archaeologists, through no fault of their own, did not know them.

When large-scale developments in the modern world have used classical architecture to assert the presence and order of the state, the politics have tended to be imperialistic, and have wanted to make a link with the Roman Empire's grandeur. This produces polarised reactions. If we broadly support the regime concerned, then – if the architecture is humanely conceived and well executed – we can see it as celebratory and appropriately grand. If we feel oppressed by the regime then we feel something quite different, as the imported classical models suppress indigenous ways of doing buildings and feel intrusive and domineering.

In Rome itself the real oppression of the Roman Empire is a thing of the past, and we can imagine ourselves more easily alongside the emperor than alongside a captive slave, because the ideas of the ruling élite are the whole of Roman literature. The slaves vastly outnumbered their masters, but they had no access to the leisure that made writing possible, so their views have to be imagined – reconstructed from very scant evidence such as graffiti – if they are going to be in the picture at all, and usually in fact they have been ignored. So a modern visitor to the Colosseum does feel oppressed or threatened by it, as they might have done when it was active. Had they been ancient Roman citizens they might have gone for the spectacle and been thrilled by it. Had they been brought there as a slave from a recently conquered province, then they might have been put to death there and the emotions would have been altogether different.

Similarly there are aesthetic responses to places such as EUR and the surviving classical buildings of the Nazi era in Berlin where the historical distance is much less – and if the threat of fascism seems real and menacing, then that can take over as the important response to the building, and the production of those feelings is the real and significant effect of the building.

Liberty and Coercion

John Ruskin, writing in the nineteenth century, preferred Gothic architecture to classical because the individual craftsman had more leeway to improvise and freely express the idea embodied in the stone. In a Gothic building each capital could be different from the others in the building, maybe through representing leaves of a tree or a scene from the Bible. By contrast he saw the use of a limited canon of orders as repetitive and coercive. Once a capital had been selected for a temple, it would be repeated exactly for the whole set for the building. What made the Gothic work better was that it gave a more immediate connection between the genius of the craftsman and its expression in the finished building.

What Ruskin had in mind here was something more like the neoclassical approach to classical design – getting it right. The kind of classical architecture that invites the kind of invention and proliferation that is there in the medieval world in the Gothic style, is present also in the classical tradition where it tends to be called baroque, but Ruskin seems to have been blind to that aspect of it and lumped it in with Renaissance architecture as haughty and inhuman. Ruskin made a correlation between the working conditions of the artisan and the merit of the architectural style, so it becomes a moral statement that Gothic is better than classical – not so much a preference as an insistence that it is right.

A generation before him Richard Payne Knight had made a similar argument, but working in exactly the opposite direction – an argument for the moral and artistic excellence of Greek work. He was thinking about the ancient temples on Sicily, which were built, he asserted, by local people, who produced outstanding work because they were free and could put all their energies into following their own impulses – so on Sicily one finds ancient, small, independent communities producing work that equals and exceeds what the greatest tyrants could commission.

Moreover he detected a falling-off in quality when the politics became imperial and subjugated the freedom of the people who were doing the creative work. He felt that when we look at ancient Greek work we see the products of unfettered genius. There was nothing comparable before, so there was no affectation. They looked at nature and took what they needed from the forms of people and plants, in a completely unaffected way – without mannerism or the intervention of received ideas about what art should be. It is a view that is difficult to defend now that we know rather more about the chronology of the works involved. Knight's thinking was inspired by Winckelmann, who could write inspiringly about what he saw, and thought that what he saw was from ancient Greece. It was usually ancient Greece at one remove.

Nevertheless this is an inspiring vision of the classical – seeing it as correct because it was in tune with good principles and not separate from nature. The aim here is not to copy the form of the ancient work, but to be inspired in the same way, so that one unaffectedly produces something equivalent given the current state of society and of our knowledge. The aim is to become Ictinus, working on the temple at Bassae, and inventing harmonious new forms of capital.

Too often classicism has become a matter of attaching ready-made standard ornament – ordering a set of precast Corinthian columns is not at all the same thing as carving them from cubic blocks of stone, finding their form within the block, and nuancing its symbolism for the building in hand. Of course the latter is much more extravagant in time and workmanship – especially before the advent of power tools – but in older buildings it is what was done. If we think we can do something equivalent without going to so much trouble, then we are deceiving ourselves.

It meant that a building that was decorated with such columns had to be important. It was not only a matter of personal taste, but of societal significance.

In the world of industrial production there is no direct link between elaborate decoration and exorbitant cost. The general look of a classical façade can be made without great outlay, from mass-produced elements. The standardised canonic orders lend themselves to mechanical reproduction, and they can be added to an otherwise plain shell of a building. That sort of thing does little to impress and can easily look like kitsch – giving the look of a sketchy imitation of something that might once have been worthwhile. Classical buildings can be built well with fine craftsmanship and then they can impress rather more, but often the classical architecture to be found in recent buildings seems to have as its aim not a creative re-thinking of what that classical might be, but a reproduction of an earlier version of classicism, so the new building seems to have arrived directly from the eighteenth century.

The point of building in a deliberately old-fashioned way can be a means to lay claim to the social prestige associated with old money, when an actual old building is unavailable or unsuitable. It might not work, and it certainly does nothing to advance the cause of art, but such a building can nevertheless bring contentment to its owner. There is a role in the world for buildings that make a place to live without making a claim to the advancement of thinking on any topic at all. Ordinary decent buildings are not highly original, and no one expects them to be. They make no claim on a place in a historical narrative. They are part of the background, while the architectural historian tends to focus on the buildings that bring about change.

Innovations

Classical architecture can be pressed into service when an old-fashioned building is demanded, and it might look as if it could have been designed in the eighteenth century or the sixteenth. It is rarer to find it used in a way that tries to be innovative, but for example at the Piazza d'Italia in New Orleans in 1978, Charles Moore produced a monumental public fountain for the city's Italian community that evokes the monumental public fountains of Italy in a colourful and fragmented way, evoking Roman ruins as well as the lively splashing waters, and using neon lighting strips to accentuate the main forms (Fig. 111). In some cases the capitals are made of folded polished steel sheets, and water jets are used to give the general effect of acanthus leaves and the reeds in reeded columns. There is inventiveness on display, and the mood is playful, not authoritarian in the least.

There is a similar mood in the kitchen of Charles Jencks's Cosmic House, where spoons are fixed on running panels, to give the effect of a Doric frieze with the three spoons per panel turning into triglyphs. These buildings use materials that seem ephemeral compared with the masonry of ancient buildings. Jencks's house is now a museum, so the delicate decoration will be conserved and will last longer than might be expected, but the robustness of the stone frieze from Bassae meant that it survived neglect and the collapse of more than one civilisation, to

be rediscovered in the nineteenth century and once again admired.

What these modern (or post-modern) works do is to reimagine classical ornament in a way that is light-hearted and could never be pressed into service as an expression of power. They would have been useless to Mussolini. That is important here, because without work like this the classical architecture of the twentieth-century dictators might have established a seemingly inevitable link between classical architecture and Fascism. The link is there, but it is not the only one. Even in modern times classical architecture can be used in ways that have nothing sinister or coercive about them.

There is no need to reimagine classical architecture every time it is used. Some of the reimagining has already been done for us. A twenty-first-century classical building is not interchangeable with an ancient building. Take the library that Thomas Beeby designed in 1987 for downtown Chicago – a prominent site. It uses a steel frame that is not expressed. At pavement level there is rugged, rusticated stonework, and the more refined decoration higher up the building includes swags that seem to be a deliberate reference to the Sainte-Geneviève Library in Paris. Then above the cornice level there are acroteria that

Fig. 111 Charles Moore, Piazza d'Italia, New Orleans (completed 1978).

broadly follow an ancient Greek precedent, but here they are modelled in sheet material and have become huge – more than a storey high. Something that size on the Parthenon would look menacing, but here the street is relatively narrow and the decoration is seen very obliquely, so it does not seem so over-scaled as the historical precedents would make us expect. Nevertheless it takes an element that is an almost negligible detail of ancient classicism and makes it loom large in the modern design.

More often modern designers take their cue from Semper's understanding of the tectonic frame – as we have seen above with David Chipperfield's work in Berlin. Demetri Porphyrios has written on Semper and makes use of disciplined masses with regular rhythms in his buildings, often with precise classical ornament at significant points such as entrances, finding common ground between the discipline of commercial practice and a self-effacing approach to urban design.

John Outram has taken a different approach, developing his designs with reference to a mythology that he has invented himself, but which makes inferences from the world as we know it, informed by readings of ancient texts (Fig. 112). For example he reminds us that Vitruvius saw the columns of classic buildings as people: the Doric column was a sturdy soldier, the Ionic column an elegant mature woman, the Corinthian a slim maiden. Their proportions encoded the different types of human figure, giving the different orders connotations of strength, grace and elegance. The image was made literal and explicit in the Caryatid porch of the Erechtheion, but in Outram's imagination it is to be understood as implied in every column.

Seen in this way the columns standing round a temple become a phalanx of guardians, protecting the cult statue of the god within. We see a version of the arrangement when a head of state moves in a procession, with guards in attendance in a geometric formation – maybe translated in the modern world into an armoured car with motorcycle outriders, two in front, two behind, staking out a moving territory that is in effect a sanctuary for the high-status person at the heart of it all.

Outram's vision is particularly compelling at the scale of the city, where – inspired by the things one sees in modern Rome – one can infer that there was a primordial Arcadian landscape at the level of the cornices of the city buildings. As one looks out across the city one sees the planted terraces of penthouse apartments and trees on distant hills, and

Fig. 112 John Outram, Temple of Storms, Stormwater Pumping Station, Isle of Dogs, London (1986–88).

the landscape does indeed seem to continue across the densely developed apartment blocks of the city centre. The narrow streets are gorges that divide up this primordial landscape, as though eroded away by rivers. The evidence for this are the cobbled streets, which look like dried-up river beds, and the fact that the blocks are called 'insulae' – islands. At one level the description is personal whimsy, but at another it touches on something much more profound, as it gives us a way to see that we are all already living in a classical landscape, and that invites us to articulate that in the small part of the city that comes under our immediate control.

There is no need to build grandiose projects to live in a way that is informed by an understanding of classical architecture. It is possible to build primitive huts and imagine the origins of architecture, or – at the most minimal extreme – just be inspired by the immediate spontaneity of Winckelmann's version of the ancient Greeks, to look around, see the traces of the classical world around one, in people who are in touch with the world and unaffectedly respond to it, in buildings here and there perhaps, but more importantly in clouds and trees and ancient sunlight, in the organic and inorganic processes that we can harness to make our lives more livable, and which, like an invisible mycelium, can make connections that unexpectedly produce epiphanies here and there. Those are the dots one needs to join as new constellations take shape and the emergent vision comes into focus.

acanthus A plant with broad leaves that grows wild around the Mediterranean. Its leaves are the basis of the Corinthian capital, where they would normally be sculpted in stone.

acroterion A decoration at the top of a Greek temple (plural: acroteria) properly at the top of the pediment, but it is also used as the name for decorations at the corners of the building seen against the sky. There they are more precisely called 'acroteria angularia' (pairing a Greek noun with a Latin adjective).

altar In an ancient temple this is an outdoor place associated with a temple, where animals were killed as sacrifices to the gods. In a Christian church it is an indoor table where the Eucharist is celebrated with bread and wine.

architrave *See* entablature.

basilica Originally a basilica was royal stoa, but in the Roman empire it became a type of official building, presided over by a statue of the emperor. The most impressive of them, in Rome, had a high central space that could be lit by clerestory windows, and lower spaces at the sides. When Christianity became an official religion of the Roman empire, the basilica presided over by an image of Christ was adopted as the form for large church buildings.

capital The top part of a column (from the word for a head in Latin: 'caput').

cathedral A church with a bishop's throne in it. 'Cathedra' is a Latin word for chair.

cella The enclosed room in a classical temple in which the cult-statue was housed. Normally it had a single door of monumental scale through which the statue could 'look' at the outdoor altar.

church A building used for Christian worship. A small church is called a chapel. Large churches (such as cathedrals) often have chapels within them, with their own altars. Alberti in his writings called churches 'temples', suggesting continuity with the ancient past. That is an unusual usage, but in modern French 'temple' is routinely used for non-Catholic places of worship.

clerestory Windows placed high up that let light into a space without giving a view out (except of sky), usually above the height of the roof of a lower part of the building. The word has an old English root, so it should be pronounced as 'clear storey'.

cornice *See* entablature.

entablature The part of a classical building above the columns. This is normally divided into three bands: 1) the **architrave**, which is plain and is a beam spanning from one column to the next; 2) the **frieze**, which can be decorated; 3) the **cornice**, which is at the top and overhangs a little. If the columns are like table legs, then the entablature is the actual table.

flute A groove in the shaft of a column. They are relatively shallow concave grooves in the case of Doric columns, and relatively narrow, deep and more tightly curved in other cases. Exacting craftsmanship is needed to cut them precisely. They would normally be cut once the stone drums of a column were in place, to make sure that the ridges aligned exactly.

frieze *See* entablature.

metope A sculpted panel in a Doric frieze (*see* entablature above). They alternate with triglyphs, which are rectangular panels (taller than they are wide) divided into three. They are quite abstract. The metopes, on the other hand, can have sculpted decoration and were more or less square. The metopes from the Parthenon are particularly famous. There were ninety-two of them, and they show scenes in which two figures are locked in a fight – some of the figures are Amazons, some of them centaurs, and the others are heroic young Greeks.

order The 'orders of architecture' are the systems of columns and beams that developed in ancient Greece and codified later. The 'canonic orders' are Doric, Ionic and Corinthian. The five orders of architecture detailed by Vignola are these three, plus Tuscan and Composite. The Doric order has fluted columns, a simple capital, and a frieze of metopes and triglyphs. The Ionic order has more flutes, a sculpted base, and a capital with two scrolls (volutes) above which the frieze runs continuously without interruption. The Corinthian order is similar to the Ionic, but the columns are more slender and the capital is decorated with stylised acanthus leaves. It was invented in Greece, but was used far more often by the Romans. The Composite order is a further enrichment developed by the Romans that combines the Ionic and Corinthian capitals. The Tuscan order is another Roman development, but this time in the direction of simplification: the columns are unfluted. They have capitals like the Doric, but bases that are more like Ionic and the other columns. Any of the orders where the columns are unfluted can be described as 'Roman' – often meaning Roman style, rather than actually ancient. So for example there is a Roman Doric order, which uses Tuscan columns to support an entablature with a Doric frieze. In addition to these canonic orders and their variants there are more idiosyncratic inventions for individual buildings. So although the orders seem very straightforward and limited in a simplified description, actually they turn out to be flexible with room for invention.

palace A grand dwelling with a number of rooms designed for display. A royal palace will include a throne room, and other spaces designed to show the monarch in a position of power. The palaces of the rich and powerful have 'state rooms' where a head of state could visit or be accommodated.

pilaster A decorative version of a column, with no structural role. A pilaster looks like a column, but it is modelled in low relief on the wall.

sanctuary A designated sacred place. It can be the interior of a building, but in the ancient world it was an open space defined by a perimeter of some sort. In Athens, for example, the agora was a sanctuary. So was the whole of the Acropolis, on which several buildings stood, with open space between them. Similarly at Epidauros the sanctuary space included the theatre (as well as temples that have perished).

stoa In ancient Greece this is a long narrow building, open on one long side with a row of columns on that side. The porch-like internal space was shaded and sheltered and could be used for anything from selling goods to teaching philosophy. Stoas sometimes have a run of smaller rooms along one side, which could be used as dining rooms, and such stoas were built in important sanctuaries where sacrifices were made (and then eaten). The Stoa of Attalos at the edge of the Athenian agora had two storeys. In modern Athens a stoa is a shopping arcade, often with a place to eat within it.

style The Greek word for a column (stili) turned into English. This is the root word for many terms that are used in descriptions of ancient temples. For example if it has six columns across the entrance front it is called 'hexastyle'. If (like the Parthenon) it has eight, then it can be called 'octastyle' or 'octostyle'. When columns go all the way round a building then the run of columns is called a 'peristyle'. When a building has no columns it can be called 'astylar'.

stylobate The base of a Greek temple – usually with three steps – on which the columns stand.

triglyph *See* metope above.

villa An ancient Roman villa was a farmstead, including outbuildings and accommodation for agricultural workers (slaves) as well as the principal dwelling. Later, for example in the Veneto, where the noble Venetian families had their estates, a villa would similarly be a rural building used in connection with agricultural production. In the case of the grand villas by Palladio, the family that owned the rural estate would also have a palace in Venice. A post-Renaissance villa is supposed not to be a principal residence.